Effecting Change

Intervention *for* Culturally *and* Linguistically Diverse Learners

Author
Almitra L. Berry, Ed.D.
Foreword
Gamal D. Brown

SHELL EDUCATION

Publishing Credits

Dona Herweck Rice, *Editor-in-Chief*; Lee Aucoin, *Creative Director;*
Don Tran, *Print Production Manager;* Timothy J. Bradley, *Illustration Manager;*
Conni Medina, *Editorial Director;* Sara Johnson, M.S.Ed., *Senior Editor;* Hillary Wolfe, *Editor;*
Lee Aucoin, *Cover Designer;* Juan Chavolla, *Interior Layout Designer;*
Corinne Burton, M.A.Ed., *Publisher*

Shell Education

5301 Oceanus Drive
Huntington Beach, CA 92649-1030
http://www.shelleducation.com
ISBN 978-1-4258-0666-8
©2011 Shell Educational Publishing, Inc.

Table of Contents

Foreword

· ·

Dr. Almitra Berry embraces the responsibility to expand teaching and learning so that it engages practitioners in the art of making students smarter. Providing alternative programmatic options to increase scholarly readiness and higher-order thinking strategies for both student and teacher demonstrates her exuberance for her chosen discipline.

Dr. Berry's body of work places significant emphasis on maximizing the academic performance of individual learners, while giving notable consideration to their readiness, learning aptitudes, and skill levels. She demonstrates that, without appropriate assessment and knowledge of individual learners, the educational process is crippled at best—and is completely ineffective at worst. Dr. Berry further establishes that cultural, social, and emotional developments are variables that must be considered and acknowledged when planning and implementing curriculum to facilitate student growth: An effective course of study must allow the institution to move from "factory models" to educational models that are progressive and individualized; and, the institution must continually test its commitment to advance these progressive initiatives.

Dr. Berry's research serves as a "how-to guide" for lifting the veil of insensitivity and reclusion, and provides the educational community a significant tool to progress the student, while bolstering educator capacity. In light of this work, educators are wise to ask themselves two critical questions when examining curricula: Does the curricula preserve existing inequalities? Is knowledge being evenly distributed? The aforementioned is the mantel that Dr. Berry has successfully articulated in *Effecting Change: Intervention for Culturally and Linguistically Diverse Learners*—to respond to all inequities, and to move toward the eradication of every faulty practice that perpetuates said inequities.

It is with great pleasure that I introduce this timely publication on educational reform and literacy intervention, as it will assist all educators in their efforts to change schools and improve education for those that need it most.   As a response to our national need for the improvement of reading instruction, this work challenges everything from teaching methods to learning assessments—while showing us how our frames of reference impact our ability to teach. Dr. Berry shows us how effective intervention can improve literacy in this country and instill in our educators the tools and processes needed for high academic achievement in the populations that they serve.

—Gamal D. Brown
Educational Consultant for Detroit, New Orleans, and
Philadelphia School systems

Introduction

· ·

Many practitioners work with culturally and linguistically diverse learners (CLDLs). I hope to help them understand not only how, but why we must differentiate instruction for students from high poverty, diverse cultures, and diverse languages so they have greater opportunities for high academic success. Use this if you are working on your own, or as part of a professional learning community to guide the evaluation, development, and monitoring of a Response to Intervention (RTI) implementation at a school site or school district. Sociopolitical debate will not prepare our children for success. Appropriate practice will.

> *"According to the latest National Assessment of Adult Literacy report (NAAL), over 90 million (4 out of 10) U.S. adults are living lives socially and economically disadvantaged due to poor reading skills. Adults with low levels of literacy are significantly more likely to live in poverty, engage in crime and other forms of social pathology, and to live unhealthy, and even shorter lives."*
>
> **—Children of the Code**
> http://www.childrenofthecode.org 2010

No matter what role you serve in the pre-K through grade 12 educational setting, you have an impact on the lives of children. You are accountable. This book presents a model and a rationale for intervention for culturally and linguistically diverse learners at risk for reading failure and/or referral to special education. I do not offer a "cookie-cutter" or "one-size-fits-all" approach. This book asks you to think—to examine your current practices and evaluate their effectiveness for the students you teach. It is imperative to understand the subtle differences in the ways children from diverse cultures and languages learn. This book will address the spectrum of understanding that is necessary to effectively design intervention for culturally and linguistically diverse students.

Chapter 1 shows how tapping into our own background and culture creates a frame of reference for culturally and linguistically diverse learners. In **Chapter 2**, we show the different approaches to reading instruction to better examine your own teaching methods and make an informed decision as to which approach is best for your students. Then, **Chapter 3** helps you understand the structure of intervention to provide context for your teaching.

Assessment is a tricky area. **Chapter 4** walks you through the ins and outs of progress monitoring, and more importantly, tells you how to act on the information and data you collect. The first and best form of intervention is prevention. **Chapter 5** outlines how strong and effective core instruction can make a huge difference.

If the core program is not meeting students' needs and they are still struggling below grade level, intervention must become more targeted. **Chapter 6** shows how to determine the kinds of interventions needed for those students who require extra help.

When your struggling learners are also challenged by cultural or language differences, what special knowledge do you need to help these students reach benchmarks? **Chapter 7** provides some answers.

Although teaching is a creative endeavor, struggling learners cannot afford to experience untested curriculum. **Chapter 8** explains why instruction must be deliberate and intentional to help these students succeed. **Chapter 9** outlines why intervention must be supported schoolwide. Collaboration among peers, colleagues, parents, and community members will be instrumental to a successful intervention implementation. Finally, we reaffirm the necessity for intervention with a morale-building **Chapter 10** that reminds you of the impact your teaching will have on the lives of your students.

Chapter 1

Building and Activating Our Own Schema

We are a culturally diverse society. Culturally and linguistically diverse learners have distinct characteristics and learning disabilities. Educators often cite this fact as one of their most difficult challenges. This book provides the foundation for a culturally appropriate response to intervention model. If properly implemented, schools can reduce the number of inappropriate referrals to special education services and allow a greater number of students, specifically students of diverse cultures and language backgrounds, to remain in the general education population while receiving appropriate instruction. Failure to respond to intervention must be correctly documented, and the use of appropriate, valid and reliable assessment measures must be employed to continually adjust instruction and reduce the referral rate. Unfortunately, the procedural demands of this process are often overlooked in credential programs.

Who Are Culturally and Linguistically Diverse Learners, and Why Do They Need Different Instruction?

First, we must define culture. Simply defined, culture is the information, norms, values, behaviors, and morals of a group. But this simplistic definition fails to address the specifics: What information? Which norms, values, and behaviors? Who determines them? Whose morals, and what are they? The culture of an ethnic group varies from one neighborhood to another, and even from one household to another. So, before we move forward on this journey, take a moment to examine your own beliefs about culture. By the end of this chapter, you may start to notice your beliefs being challenged. Philosophically, culture is socially, not genetically, transmitted. It is porous, changing, influenced internally and externally, and likely to contain subcultures that stray from the original culture. Culture and subculture exist as essential elements that cannot be disregarded in today's classrooms. Yes, culture is comprised of the norms, values, behaviors, and morals common to a group. Each person may participate and operate in multiple cultures over the course of any day. Think of your own school. The culture of your school may be distinctly different from the culture of your classroom, your home, your extended family, and the families of your students.

Functionalists believe that educational systems exist to propagate the accepted culture of a society. So, there must be some agreement on which values, norms, morals, attitudes, and behaviors should be transferred to the students, especially if those students do not share the broader society's culture. Others question whether a consensus even exists in American society, and if there is any type of societal consensus about core values.

The topic of culture becomes more important when talking about the culture of marginalized groups such as ethnic minorities, language minorities, and students of lower socioeconomic status. When a group compares its knowledge of purpose, general knowledge, and influences to society as a whole, those marginalized groups tend to create an identity that is socially unique (Pai, Adler, and Shadiow 2005). Multiple cultures may exist in your classroom. Some see this as a good thing, others see it as a challenge. For teaching and learning, a multicultural environment presents both unique opportunities and challenges.

You and your students must be able to adjudicate through cross-cultural conflicts in a society that is undergoing rapid social changes. Whatever our culture or cultures, our norms, rituals, and traditions may be attacked or ridiculed—but they are still ours. Your students have theirs. As they learn to operate in ours, we must accept theirs and add to it what will be beneficial, without removing that which is valuable and necessary for them to operate in their home environments. This requires that we learn to look at students through a variety of lenses. We have to get out of our comfort zones. We must transcend culture in order to be effective. The comprehension of the culture of school and the culture of students' homes is essential to success—our success in teaching, and their success in learning. One component of the socio-cultural process involves the acquisition of a second language at school. The core of acquisition incorporates all the surrounding social and cultural processes that occur through everyday life within the student's past, present, and future and in all contexts. These contexts include home, school, community, and society. For example, at school, the instructional environment in a class structure may create social and psychological distance between groups. Community or social patterns such as prejudice and discrimination expressed towards groups or individuals in personal contexts can influence student achievement in school as well as societal problems. Negative patterns can strongly influence a student's response to the new language (Tozer, Violas, and Senese 2002). Hopefully this book will help you question your beliefs about the purpose of education and the practices you were taught. Through questioning, you may see the purpose of school very differently than when you were a beginning teacher.

This book sets forth a practical, socio-culturally relevant approach to intervention. Think of the classroom as its own unique culture, comprised of students whose cultural reality is both independent of and external to the reality of school. Teaching and learning must be based on the recognition that an alternate reality exists in the lives of many, if not all, of our students. The culturally and linguistically diverse student may not be able to transcend his or her situation. However, they create schemata from experiences both within and outside of school that may be used to solve problems in all of the students' environments.

Consider the many different contexts, the varying environments, circumstances, and perspectives that children face in their day-to-day lives. School imparts a culture, a perspective, and a set of norms. School provides a model for students to carry into the larger context of society. So, it seems to be a good idea to establish a universal set of core standards for behavior and decision making. That core set of standards rests on readily accepted beliefs about "good" and "bad" practices. This is necessary from a legal standpoint, because we must protect children. It is also necessary from an ethical perspective, because what is unethical (while not necessarily illegal) might harm children. At the same time, we have to take into account the ethical code of the students' home culture. It may conflict with the core set of standards we apply at school. As educators, then, we must approach our students with an understanding of our differences and strive to create a balance. We must view each student through two frames: we must see them as they exist within our classrooms, and we must see them as they realistically must function in their home environment.

Plato taught that good and bad can only be comprehended from within the context of a particular social order. Moral behavior at home might be immoral behavior in the school. For example, cheating—an unethical behavior at school—may be viewed as collaborative community building by students from another culture. If a cultural moral code states that the duty an intelligent child is to provide assistance to those who may struggle academically, then goodness follows from teaching a peer. But in most of our classrooms, there is a fine line between peer-to-peer teaching and cheating; this is a line that may be unintentionally crossed by a student from a different home culture, unless that boundary is clearly defined by the teacher.

Aristotle taught that good and bad are based on the relationship between natural laws and man's laws. So, in this context, a student would view cheating as a negative thing only if there were expressed rules governing the behavior, and only if the students helped to establish the rules. If the rules of the classroom stated that students were to assist their peers as a way to contribute to society, then the behavior would be ethical. If the students did not help to create the rules, however, then they will not internally view those rules as applicable or relevant. The code of home and the code of school must be recognized and valued, or we risk losing the respect of the whole child by ignoring a significant part.

What Is Linguistic Diversity?

What is your definition of linguistic diversity? This question is not easily answered. When you think of linguistic diversity, do you consider those students who speak only English, but whose English is not strong enough to engage in deep conversation because they lack the vocabulary to articulate their thoughts? Does your definition include English-only speakers who have grammatical and syntactical patterns that do not adhere to the conventions of school English? If so, great! You are on the right track. If not, take a minute to broaden your scope. Often, we think of English language learners as a group of children identified as such based on a test. School systems around the country have many different labels for these students and the instructional programs they receive. The most common acronyms and terms and what they mean are shown in the chart below:

Common Acronyms and Terms and Their Definitions	
0.5 Lingual	Students who are neither proficient in their home language nor in school English (also, *semilingual*).
AAVE (African American Vernacular English)	The distinct, complex, and rule-governed linguistic system featuring semantic and syntactic conventions expressed in patterns divergent from school English (SE).
CLDL (Culturally and Linguistically Diverse Learner)	Learners who come from homes whose cultures are not mainstream, middle-class, Anglo American and/or who come from language backgrounds other than school English.
ELD (English Language Development)	Instruction in the listening, speaking, reading, writing, and thinking domains of the English language; usually designed for English language learners from non-English based home languages.
ELL (English Language Learner)	The student, usually identified and rated by formal assessment, who comes to school with a home language other than school English.
ESOL (English Speakers of Other Languages)	See *ELL*.
FEP (Fluent English Proficient)	A student whose English is sufficient to participate in instruction without specialized or scaffolded instruction.
IFEP (Initially Fluent English Proficient)	Identified ELLs who enter school with fluent English although they come from a home where other than English is spoken.

Common Acronyms and Terms and Their Definitions *(cont.)*	
LM **(Language Minority)**	A student whose primary language is not the majority (English) language.
LEP **(Limited English Proficient)**	A student whose English is limited to the point where they cannot fully participate in English instruction without support, scaffolded instruction, or targeted intervention for language development.
NEP **(Non-English Proficient)**	A student whose English is so limited that it precludes accessing mainstream instruction. (See also *newcomer*.)
Newcomer	A student who has no comprehension of English; generally, a new arrival to the United States.
Redesignee	A student whose proficiency in English has risen to the point that they are no longer non- or limited in English, but rather fluent English proficient.
SE **(School/Standard English)**	The linguistic system that is spoken in schools, featuring the grammar, usage, and mechanics of the English language accepted as the standard for textbook instruction.
SEL **(School/Standard English Leaner)**	A student learning the English of school even though their home language may be English.
Semilingual	Students proficient neither in their home language nor school English. (See also *0.5 Lingual.*)

Think again about the question, "Who are English language learners?" Often overlooked are some Native Americans, some African Americans, and some students of poverty who come to school lacking a strong grasp of school English (SE), even though English may be the only language they know. They do not take the language assessments that would classify them as English language learners because they do not have a foreign language background.

Educators need to understand the differences among students in order to create a more culturally congruent classroom. The cultural differences theory takes a classroom-level view so teachers can understand the factors that lead to low achievement among minority students. This book will assist you in creating a classroom that provides the highest possible academic achievement for all students. Also discussed is the labor market theory of Ogbu (1987) that includes the global and cultural elements that cause system-wide suppression of academic achievement for culturally and linguistically diverse learners (CLDLs). By blending these two theories, this book offers a perspective that will be useful for the classroom teacher, the instructional leader at a school site, or for a district-wide study of the educational system.

Effective instruction for children from culturally and linguistically diverse backgrounds calls for a variety of instructional activities and other strategies. Those strategies, activities, and methodologies require us to take the children's diversity of experience into account.

Many of the important educational innovations in current practice, such as flexible- and mixed-age grouping, are the direct result of teachers who have adapted instruction to meet the challenges posed by teaching children from diverse backgrounds. It is vital that teachers be cognizant of how a student's home and home culture experiences affect his or her values, patterns of language use, and interpersonal style. Children are likely to be more responsive to a teacher who is sensitive to their culture and its behavioral patterns.

Major Demographics Impacting Schools and Classrooms Today

Educational journals, blogs, and various websites all consistently report on one demographic pattern: the fastest growing population in America's schools are linguistically diverse students. With this diversity also comes cultural diversity. It is important to recognize those groups most frequently left behind.

Today, limited English proficient (LEP) students are the most rapidly growing population in American schools. Between 1993 and 2003, the percentage of English language learners at elementary and secondary schools increased by over 50%, from 2.8 to more than 4 million children. Many states experienced even higher growth rates of 200% or more, such as Alabama, Arkansas, Colorado, Indiana, and North Carolina (Cohen, Deterding, and Clewell 2005).

As more children with home languages other than English enter schools, more teachers will face the challenge of instructing children who have limited English language skills—an experience no longer exclusive to teachers in particular schools or geographical areas. All teachers will need to know something about how children learn a second language. Intuitive assumptions can be erroneous. Children's progress can be hindered, and they could be affected emotionally if we have unrealistic expectations or inaccurate understandings of the process of language learning and its relationship to acquiring other academic skills and knowledge. (See Chapter 7 for further discussion.)

Some historical context is needed to frame our thinking. The land we call America has never been monolingual. Native American tribes spoke hundreds of indigenous languages throughout the territory before European colonization. Spanish-speaking settlements in the Southwest not only preceded English settlements on the East Coast, but thrived throughout the Southwest, from California to Texas and as far north as Wyoming, until Mexico ceded the Southwest in 1848. Even in the 13 original colonies, German was spoken as early as 1683 when religious refugees founded Germantown, Pennsylvania.

By the late 1700s, German Americans accounted for over 8.5% of the country's European population. German was used as the language of instruction in schools throughout the states of the Midwest where a new generation of German immigrants settled (Wiley 1998). Although French speakers made up less than 1% of the population in the 1790 census, the acquisition of Louisiana in 1803 added substantially to that figure, including speakers of Cajun French and French Creóle (Gilbert 1981). In addition to the indigenous languages of the territory and the languages of European colonists and immigrants, the linguistic diversity of African slaves contributed further to the country's diverse linguistic heritage.

While America has more than twice the number of speakers of other languages (ESOL) now than in the past, the percentage of the total population is actually less: 17.9% now as compared to 24% in 1910 and 25% in 1790 (Wiley and Wright 2004). Today, however, the diversity of languages other than English spoken is greater (McKay and Wong 2000). Despite this multilingual, multicultural heritage, languages other than English have continuously been viewed as a problem or threat to national unity. From the linguistic isolation of African slaves and forced assimilation and isolation of Native Americans during westward expansionism, to the Americanization campaign of the early to mid-20th century, we have endeavored to acculturate and linguistically assimilate a culturally and linguistically diverse population.

The Civil Rights movement of the 1960s impacted the general prejudice against languages other than English through policy, and perhaps popularly as well. One gain made during this era was in the education of children from language minority groups. Their educational needs up to that point were neglected and their native language skills were at best considered irrelevant or at worst were brutally repressed. The results of this mistreatment included elevated dropout rates, lower academic achievement, and fewer college-bound students and college graduates (Wiley and Wright 2004). Civil rights groups and parents pressured school systems to reconsider the total immersion approach—popularly known as "sink-or-swim"—that dominated the educational experience of students with limited English proficiency. This occurred through lawsuits, student boycotts, and increased involvement in the political process.

When President George W. Bush introduced the No Child Left Behind Act (NCLB) in 2001, he echoed the sentiment of President Lyndon Baines Johnson's introduction of the Elementary and Secondary Education Act (ESEA) in 1965. Both presidents referenced the discouraging plight of some children: the African American, Hispanic, urban, and the poor. In 1965 and even today, these are still the children the American educational system holds back and leaves behind. These are the children most often discarded as "uneducable, under-educable, learning disabled, having special needs, and a host of other categories" as we rationalize their poor academic performance (Gant 2005). Education remains the most viable route from poverty. Every child merits education.

A student's self-concept is strongly affected by the value teachers and student peers place on the use of various languages. For effective learning to take place, a student needs to have a positive self-concept. As teachers, if our words or deeds indicate to a student that his or her primary language is wrong or incorrect, the learner's self-confidence is diminished, and might hinder their ability to learn (Tozer, Violas, and Senese 2002).

During the past 20 years, rapidly increasing language minority demographics have had a major impact on our schools. There have been varied instructional approaches that educators have undertaken to address the concern for providing a meaningful education for language minority students, but many of us are still struggling to identify the most effective educational practices. A great deal of misunderstanding occurs because many policy-makers—as well as educators—assume that language learning can be isolated from other issues, and that non-native speakers of English must learn English before learning anything else. Not only is this an overly simplistic perception, it does not work. Four specific groups of students continue to show historically poor academic performance:

- African American
- Latino American
- recent immigrants
- students of poverty (Title I eligible)

In 1992, 25% of English language learners in high poverty schools had repeated at least one grade level. In 1987, the U.S. Department of Education found that African Americans made up 12% of the general student population, but 24% of the special education population. Between 1976 and 1994, the percentage of Hispanic children identified as learning disabled increased from 24% to 51%.

Fast-forward to the present. Today, the 20 largest U.S. school districts are disproportionately minority in composition—65%—with disproportionately higher poverty levels (KewalRamani et al 2007). Balfanz and Legters (2004) found, "A majority minority high school is five times more likely" to promote less than 40% of incoming freshmen to senior status in four years. Lower socioeconomic status children enter school with language deficits, which translate to reading deficits, resulting in the achievement gaps prevalent in large urban districts (Wise et al. 2007).

As an instructional coach, I have often heard teachers complain that the parents were not pulling their weight in educating their children. The data tells us part of the story. DeBell and Chapman (2006) reported only 46% of Black and 48% of Hispanic students have computer access at home, compared to 78% of White and 74% of Asian students. Only 26% of Black and Hispanic students have home access to the Internet. Further, only 39% of students eligible for Title I, compared to 76% of non-poverty students, have computer access at home; only 19% of students eligible for Title I have home Internet access (DeBell and Chapman 2006).

How can we ask the parents, many of whom have no more than a high school education, to do what we as educators are unable to do? We have not taught the children to read, write, calculate, and think. These parents are bringing us the best children they have. Just as they trust the physician to diagnose and treat their children when they are ill, they trust us to teach their children to read, write, calculate, and think. We are the trusted practitioners with the remedies for illiteracy and innumeracy.

Effective education of culturally and linguistically diverse learners affirms the values of the home culture and instills in the child a positive emotional attitude toward his or her own background (McLaughlin 1992). This means that diversity of experience is taken into account for curriculum design and delivery. Some of the innovations in Response to Intervention (RTI) in this book are the direct result of adapting instruction to meet these challenges.

A multicultural, reconstructionist education calls for classrooms that reflect and celebrates diversity. Perspectives and contributions of diverse groups should be expressed and conceptually displayed at all times across subject areas. Bilingualism or multilingualism should be endorsed. However, classroom diversity is not an excuse for lowered expectations. Every child can learn. Culturally appropriate response to intervention (CA-RTI) is a method of intervention that takes students' cultures, backgrounds, and languages into account and allow equal access to all students while building on their learning styles, cultural, and language abilities.

Conclusion

CLDLs are the fastest growing population in America's public schools; to change the life trajectories of students most at risk, we must begin with these children. Debate over the best instructional methods for these learners has been waged for some time and will likely persist. That which makes us unique also fosters cultural and linguistic diversity challenges. Therefore, we must find the best practices for teaching in terms of language of instruction, methodology, and axiology.

Reflect and Act

1. Define and describe the culture and the various languages of your classroom and your school. Identify practices that are culturally subtractive; then, eliminate those practices.

2. Revisit your definition of culture from the beginning of the chapter. Has it changed? What new understandings have you gained about cultural and linguistic diversity?

Two Theories, One Result

Why do CLDLs struggle in many of our schools? We will examine two trends that tend to surface when digging deep into instructional beliefs and practices. The first is the soft bigotry of low expectations. The second is the lack of accountability, something that has been referred to as "dysteachia" (see Children of the Code.org). For context, it will be necessary to examine the seven theories on the teaching of reading, and then to take some first steps into placing our practices on that spectrum.

Practitioner's Perspective

Doctors take a Hippocratic Oath. What would an educator's oath look like? Perhaps something like this:

I will apply pedagogic measures for the benefit of all children according to my ability and judgment; I will keep them from illiteracy and innumeracy. I will neither use an inappropriate instructional method, nor will I make a suggestion to this effect. I will not teach to a test. I will teach for the benefit of children, remaining free of all intentional injustice, of all mischief, and in particular of low expectations for students who come to learn.

(adapted from Lasagne's modern translation of the Hippocratic Oath 1964)

This book will not address value ethics. However, it works from the premise that the educated populace demands the fair and equal treatment of all children, particularly the at-risk, and that instructional decision-making be based on data and proven outcomes. Hall (2008) referred to "doing harm, allowing harm, and denying resources" in the context of moral philosophy. Based on the data for at-risk students, they are being exposed to one or all three of these instructional experiences. Consequently, these students (most likely the culturally and linguistically diverse learners) require more intense intervention.

How are students being exposed to these practices? The two most prevalent ways are through the soft bigotry of low expectations and a lack of accountability by teachers: *dysteachia*. Through either or both of these practices, we are acquiescing to unacceptable outcomes for at-risk students.

The data speaks for itself. Comparisons of the 2005, 2007, and 2009 National Assessment of Educational Progress (Perie, Grigg, and Donahue 2005; Lee, Grigg, and Donahue 2007; National Center for Education Statistics 2009) indicates that at fourth grade:

- the national average reading score rose by only five points between 1992 and 2007

- there was no increase in the number of students performing at or above the basic proficiency level in reading from 1992–2007

- the percentage of children performing at or above a proficient level rose by a mere two points, from 29% to 31% in reading

Eighth-grade findings differed only in that the number of students performing at or above a Proficient level shows essentially no change from 1992. The statistics are even more grim for African-American, Hispanic, and impoverished students. At the fourth-grade level, the following percentage of students were scoring at or above the proficient level:

- 15% of African-American students

- 16% of Hispanic students

- 17% of impoverished students

By eighth-grade level, those percentages dropped:

- 13% of African-American students

- 16% of Hispanic students

- 16% of impoverished students

The white-black score gap was 26 points in 2009, compared to 31 points in 1992, prior to accommodations. Hispanics did not fare much better, with a gap of 25 points in 2009, compared to 27 points in 1992. There was no change for impoverished students from 1998 (the first time the data was tracked) to 2009, with a score gap of 26 points.

The Soft Bigotry of Low Expectations

Rod Paige, former Secretary of Education (2001–2005), was the first person to refer to "the soft bigotry of low expectations" during the launch of the No Child Left Behind Act. He asked, "Who among us would condemn a child to an inferior education? Which child? Whose child?" (Paige, in Scherer 2004). Webster's dictionary defines *bigotry* as the "obstinate and unreasoning attachment of one's own belief and opinions with narrow-minded intolerance of beliefs opposed to them." Believing that there is only one approach to teaching reading to all children is a form of bigotry. If we believe that teaching to the invisible middle is an appropriate strategy, we are expressing a form of bigotry. Both of these beliefs are dismissive of the data. Researchers into the science of teaching and learning have repeatedly validated that some instructional methods just do not work. This, believe it or not, is nothing new. In 1964, President Johnson declared a war on poverty, and viewed education for students we now call "at-risk" as a key element in winning that war. Johnson said: "There is no more senseless waste than the waste of the brainpower and skill of those who are kept from college by economic circumstance." Impoverished students in 1964 were demographically similar to students of poverty today.

Despite the research, mainstream academia still supports opinion over science when it comes to educating our most at-risk students. Here are two ways the soft bigotry of low expectations theory shows itself: Constructivism, or child-centered pedagogy, while widely researched and practiced, is not supported as the best means of instruction for students deemed at risk, particularly those who are two or more years behind. Carnine (2000) wrote of the educational establishment's strong philosophical bias toward constructivism, regardless of the results of valid, scientific research. Kim and Axelrod (2005) supported Carnine's premise citing 56% of surveyed teachers self-reported a student-centered teaching philosophy while only 15% believed it important to teach discrete skills and specific information to children regardless of outcomes.

Teachers cannot assume that at-risk students are able to discover and test their own learning. They lack sufficient schema and breadth of knowledge. Without explicit instruction they cannot make connections between concepts, because they do not have the knowledge to consider that a connection may exist. When teachers prefer a particular method of instruction, regardless of student outcomes, I would ask them to reflect on that preference. Is it serving the students, or themselves? In researching and implementing Response to Intervention (RTI), along with the increased levels of accountability and the focus of educational research on experimental methods, teachers must think beyond what is comfortable for them. They must focus on what works for students. The first way to do this is by examining the existing research based on demographically similar populations.

Taking Responsibility for Students' Achievement

The second theory permits teachers to sometimes relinquish responsibility for their students' achievement. This has been referred to as *dysteachia*. The real crime in this theory is its willful application by the teacher. When a teacher engages in practices that make learning difficult or impossible for at-risk students, including failure to employ validated methodologies that are appropriate for the learner, then the teacher is consciously denying them opportunities for progress. This amounts to "allowing of harm" (Hall 2008) since educators fail to reduce the risk status of students even though they are cognizant of their ability to do so.

As free adults and educators, we have the ability to choose our behaviors. We choose the instructional methods in our schools and classrooms. The methodology we use is selected to achieve a desired result. If this result serves our agenda but not the student's, if the methods are chosen for our convenience without regard to what is best for the student, then the motivation for teaching becomes self-serving, and thus, *dysteaching*.

The desire for achievement over accountability potentially drives *dysteachia* to the other extreme of "teaching to the test,"—or worse, blatant cheating. Desiring a specific Annual Yearly Progress (AYP) gain may tempt a teacher away from doing what is right for at-risk students. In these instances, the educator has put his or her own interests ahead of the student: it is more important to hold onto a job than to address the risk factors for the culturally and linguistically diverse learner.

A Moral Obligation Approach to Intervention

We have a moral obligation to teach the right way. Response to Intervention (RTI) provides a framework for doing so. In culturally appropriate responses to intervention (CA-RTI), the outcomes could never justify *dysteachia*. Both the ethical right and the valid science dictate the appropriate methods for teaching and learning (see figure 2.1 below). Consider CA-RTI from a perspective of just

Fig. 2.1. Appropriate Methods

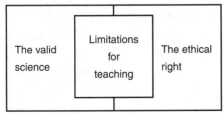

or unjust acts: *dysteachia* qualifies as an act of theft. Withdrawing appropriate academic instruction is akin to the theft of intellectual property. Those engaged in *dysteachia* are robbing children of their academic potential. To use a medical metaphor, *dysteachia* here is the same as refusing to provide insulin to a diabetic. We must move away from these practices that breed *dysteachia*.

Getting Beyond Dogma

Although research (National Reading Panel 2000) supports that 95% of all students may be taught to operate on grade level with appropriate instruction, school districts nationwide repeatedly debate the topic of student retention. Retention is one of the many factors considered in creating an accountability system for state and districts (Frey et al. 2005). The effectiveness of retention has yet to be determined; however, the ethics of social promotion surfaces as one form of student retention. Social promotion is the practice of advancing students to the next grade level based on attendance requirements, social interactions, and age rather than academic performance or the ability to meet benchmark proficiency. Through effective instruction, culturally appropriate response to intervention is designed to counter the practice of social promotion for culturally and linguistically diverse learners.

Terms such as *held back, repeating, retained,* and *left back* supposedly reduce students' anxiety about repeating a grade level (Frey et al. 2005). But to whose benefit, and to whose demise, is the practice of retaining children at grade level, or socially promoting them, if we do not change the way teaching and learning occur? If students are not promoted each year due to failure to meet benchmarks, then we as teachers should hold ourselves accountable for the failure to perform our duties. Rather than punishing the students, we should consider that the instructional approaches have failed. The disproportionate number of culturally and linguistically diverse children who are retained demonstrates our ethical breech of duty.

The Philosophy of Reading Instruction

No Child Left Behind inspired much political rhetoric and debate. But evidence is clear: scientifically-based and researched methods of instruction produce desired gains, and students are capable of learning to established benchmarks. Why can some schools close the gap when others cannot? There are many approaches to teaching and all profess to have the same outcome: skilled reading. Schunk (2004) defines skilled reading as "a complex task that involves perceptual, cognitive, and linguistic processes" as well as, "automaticity of word recognition, rather than actual recognition, distinguishes good from poor readers" (p. 400). McCardle, Scarborough, and Catts (2001) are widely cited in their definition of skilled reading as "the ability to derive meaning from text accurately and efficiently." It is difficult for some educators to articulate why they prefer one method over another, let alone articulate the theories behind their choices, or cite the necessary evidence to prove their effectiveness.

Check Yourself

- What is your preferred method of instruction?

- What are the theoretical underpinnings of your preferred method of instruction?

- Describe the quantitative, scientific evidence that supports the method you use with your students.

Seven Theories of Reading Instruction

The chart below classifies and explains seven theories of reading instruction.

Theory	Type
• Behavioral Theory	**Behavioral**
• Functional Reading Systems Theory • Theory of Automatic Sight-Word Reading	**Information Processing**
• Levels of Language Theory • Language and Literacy Theory	**Behavioral Psycholinguistic**
• Cognitive Reading Theory • Constructivist Reading Perspective	**Cognitive and Constructivist**

Behavioral Theories

Theory 1: Behavioral Theory

These theories explain learning in terms of scientific events and quantifiable data (Schunk 2004). They offer the most explicit and scripted methods for teaching reading. According to Borman et al. (2002), evidence supports the effectiveness of these direct instruction models. One subskill is mastered before another is introduced. Through constant review and practice, students master increasingly complex text with automaticity and prosody.

Teacher's Role

The teacher models explicit skill instruction and teaches content through reinforcement and corrective feedback. Failure to provide corrective feedback can result in the learning of errors (Schunk 2004). (See figure 2.2.)

Implementation

Mathes et al. (2005) and Kamps et al. (2007) found that implementation of commercial curricula produced significant gains in skilled reading in students deemed at-risk.

Fig. 2.2. Skilled Reading

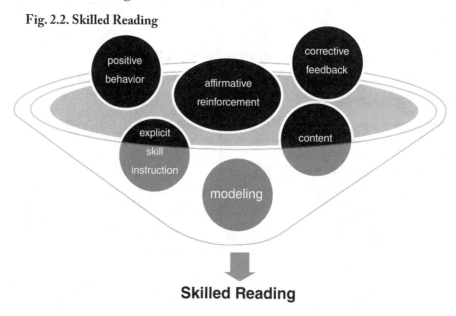

Skilled Reading

Information Processing

These theories incorporate functional reading systems and automatic sight-word reading. The learner is a processor of data inputs (Schunk 2004). There are similarities between behavorial and information processing theories, but the latter are distinguished by the focus on the mental or cognitive processes rather than external factors in the learning environment.

Theory 2: Functional Reading Systems Theory

Learning to read relies upon multiple component cognitive acts that must work concurrently (Berninger et al. 2006). Fluency and automaticity in various contexts must be addressed to achieve skilled reading. (See figure 2.3.)

Teacher's Role

Reading and comprehension skills must occur through explicit, systematic instruction from mastery of the alphabetic principle through reading to automaticity. Instruction is individualized, when necessary (Berninger et al. 2006).

Implementation

Including orthography as one of the systems being processed distinguishes this from Levels of Language Theory. Implementation would require the educator to build aural language first.

Fig. 2.3. Instructional Spectrum

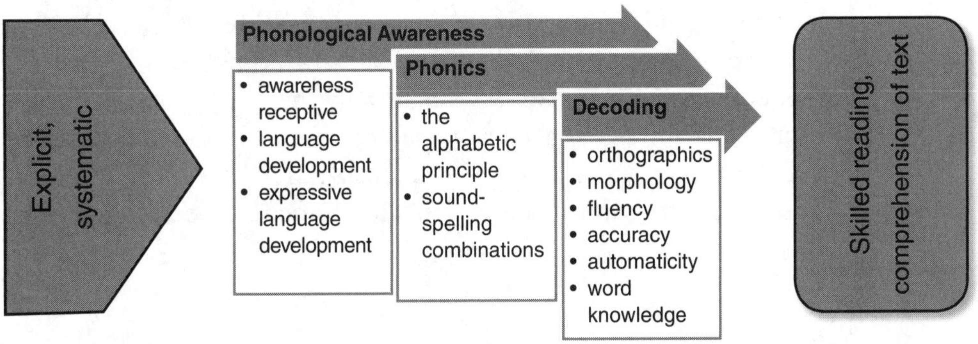

Explicit, systematic

Phonological Awareness

- awareness receptive
- language development
- expressive language development

Phonics

- the alphabetic principle
- sound-spelling combinations

Decoding

- orthographics
- morphology
- fluency
- accuracy
- automaticity
- word knowledge

Skilled reading, comprehension of text

Theory 3: Theory of Automatic Sight-Word Reading

Sight-word reading fluency is developed through whole word analysis and recognition of grapheme-phoneme (letter-sound) correspondence. Fluency in reading of connected text requires knowledge of "sublexical phonological units and their orthographic counterparts" (Speece and Ritchie 2005). Germinal experimental research on the study of response times in whole-word reading to test the theory of automatic sight-word reading as an element of skilled reading suggested that explicit instruction in grapho-phonemic awareness improved reading speed and accuracy, and generalized reading ability to unfamiliar words (Ehri and Wilce 1983). Ehri and Wilce (1983) also found that repeated practice of familiar words did not improve "unitized response levels" of familiar words in less skilled readers, nor did repeated practice improve reading speed.

Teacher's Role

Speece and Ritchie (2005) suggest teaching phonemic awareness and phonics in an explicit method to allow children facility in moving to connected text with the subskills to engage in fluent and prosodic reading. Automatic sight-word reading based on grapho-phonemic awareness and the generalization of correspondences across word types and structures should accompany the development of early word recognition and not be delayed or regarded as a "later-developing skill" (Speece and Ritchie 2005).

Implementation

Implementation in the classroom would require teachers to provide a solid foundation in phonemic awareness and phonics. Instruction would include an early introduction of grapho-phonemic awareness. Sound-spelling instruction should explicitly teach the multiple variations of spellings for each phoneme and the rules governing the spellings. Implementation recognizes that less skilled readers require a more explicit approach. (See figure 2.4.)

Fig. 2.4. Automatic Sight-Word Reading

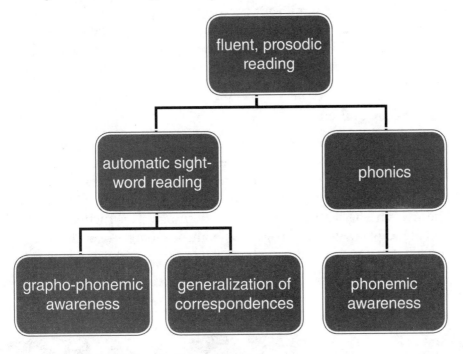

Behavioral Psycholinguistic

Levels of Literacy Theory and Language and Literacy Theory are categorized as behavioral psycholinguistic theories because implementation of either requires a behaviorist approach to teaching and learning.

Theory 4: Levels of Language Theory

Aural language is composed of multiple levels that transfer to learning to read (Berninger et al. 2006). This theory applies to the comprehension side of skilled reading, in that meaning may not be derived from printed text when a student has low verbal comprehension skills. (See figure 2.5.)

Teacher's Role

Moerk's research (Schunk 2004) indicated that others in a child's environment may assist in the development of deep structure of language and may serve the function of the language acquisition device (LAD) in a significant way. This supports the theory of language and literacy as a component of developing skilled reading in school-aged children at risk. Teachers provide the foundation, and may work with families of these students to reinforce behaviors at home.

Implementation

Phonological working memory is an important source of the differences found in learning to read among children. Studies have shown a direct relationship between word- and sentence-level working memory in tasks involving children listening to a prompt and responding either orally or in writing. Instruction that includes explicit aural language development supports later skills in decoding, comprehension, spelling, handwriting, and composition (Berninger et al. 2010).

Fig. 2.5. Levels of Language

Theory 5: Language and Literacy Theory

Myers and Botting (2008) reiterate that reading is comprised of two elements: decoding of print and comprehension.

Fig. 2.6. Listening and Reading

Across skill levels, decoding of print correlates with the phonological skills of phonemic awareness and phonics (National Reading Panel 2000). Comprehension additionally relies on verbal ability, spoken language competence, and capacity to engage in aural language (Hoover and Gough 1990). Biemiller (1999) wrote, "...a child's maximum level of reading comprehension is determined by the child's level of listening comprehension." (See figure 2.6.)

Teacher's Role

A bidirectional relationship exists between spoken language and literacy. This relationship is particularly important in older children where language learning inputs are increasingly text-based and lower levels of aural language and vocabulary constructs inhibit meaning-making of printed text. Increased verbal comprehension and verbal IQ through explicit oral language development facilitates increased comprehension of written language. Here are some recommendations for classroom application:

- Develop both the language and literacy environment concurrently.

- Attend to comprehension difficulties and try to determine the origin of the weakness, which may be due to expressive or receptive language limitations.

- Build language by explicitly teaching oral language for 20 to 30 minutes per day at the kindergarten to third grade level, and 30 minutes per day in grades four through six.

Implementation

Gersten and Geva (2003) suggested that with proactive teaching measures and appropriate instruction (based on a Behaviorist model of instruction) culturally and linguistically diverse learners' (CLDLs) acquisition of reading and spelling in English progresses at the same rate as non-CLDLs. Research has stressed the importance of teaching English in an explicit oral language development program to bolster the thinking skills of CLDLs and students of lower socioeconomic status for a minimum of

30 minutes per instructional day for increased comprehension of written language, as shown in figure 2.7 (Gersten and Geva 2003; Graves and Gersten 2002; Kamps et al. 2007).

Fig. 2.7. Spoken Language and Literacy

Cognitive and Constructivist

Even with the increased levels of accountability and the focus of reading research on experimental methods, I was taxed to find quantitative findings on the successful implementation of cognitive theories of reading with at-risk students. The line between cognitive theories and constructivist theories is fundamentally obscured in the research. The following paragraphs provide a framework for those present practices which subscribe to the Vygotskian and Piagetian Theories of teaching reading.

Theory 6: Cognitive Reading Theory

Cognitive theory is founded upon the concept of metacognition, or knowing about knowing (Richgels 1982). Thus, with instruction based on cognitive reading theory, children will learn to read and comprehend by being read to, thus observing the modeled process of comprehension, and applying these modeled skills to authentic activities and constructing their own knowledge. Metacognition encompasses two related sets of skills: an awareness of the skills, strategies, and resources required in reading, and proper timing and application of these skills and strategies to ensure successful completion of the task being taught (Schunk 2004).

Teacher's Role

The teacher's role in the classroom is facilitative. The teacher models strategies, makes knowledge explicit, and then coaches learners as they apply these strategies to reading activities (see figure 2.8). Teachers provide skill instruction by modeling while reading authentic literature to children. A heavy emphasis is placed on reading and literature, allowing for long, uninterrupted blocks of reading activities in a cooperative, positive classroom environment. Teachers provide ample amounts of oral reading to children and should allow them to read books of their choosing at their developmental level, while providing social interaction to facilitate learning (Frey et al. 2005; Iaquinta 2006).

Fig. 2.8. Cognitive Reading Theory

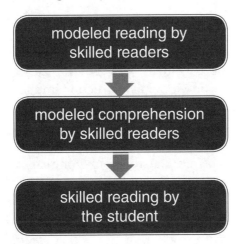

Implementation

The primary challenge with this approach in the classroom with students at risk is that assumptions may be made about levels of language, facility of language use, schema, and phonological awareness skills that are the subject of all other theories of reading (Stanovich 2004). The secondary challenge is the lack of scientific evidence that demonstrates the effectiveness of a purely cognitive approach to teaching reading.

Theory 7: Constructivist Reading Perspective

Constructivism is a meaning-based approach emphasizing comprehension and enrichment (Frey, et al. 2005). It is based on the fundamental assumption that students will create knowledge based on their existing knowledge or beliefs as they interact or come into conflict with new ideas and situations. Constructivist reading perspective contends that developing skilled reading is similar to developing oral language proficiency: reading is a natural act (Stanovich 2004). Constructivists argue that reading is learned by observing the reading of others, listening to good readers read, and engaging in reading texts of interest (Frey, et al. 2005; Iaquinta 2006). Constructivism is a meaning-based approach emphasizing comprehension and enrichment, not instruction in the discrete skills of reading.

Teacher's Role

The constructivist teacher is a coach—modeling strategies, making knowledge explicit, and guiding learners in reading activities. Teachers provide skill instruction implicitly while reading authentic literature to students (see figure 2.9). Very similar to the cognitive classroom, a substantial emphasis is placed on reading and literature, with long, uninterrupted blocks of reading activities in a cooperative, positive classroom environment.

Implementation

As in cognitive reading theory, the challenge with this approach in the classroom with students at risk is that assumptions are made about levels of language, facility of language use, schema, and phonological awareness skills that are the subject of all other theories concerning reading. The constructivist approach does not provide for instruction in the tool-based skills of reading. Similarly, scientific and quasi-scientific studies that evidence the efficacy of the model, particularly with children at risk, do not exist in the literature.

Fig. 2.9. Constructivist Method

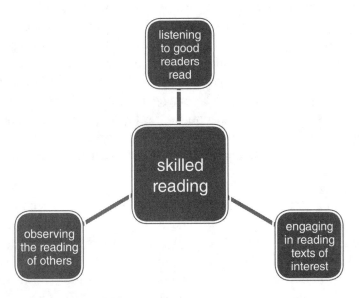

Choose the Right Approach

Much evidence, in particular The Report of the National Reading Panel (National Reading Panel 2000) and Borman et al. (2002) support the development of skilled reading in students at risk through the approaches described above as behavioral, psycholinguistic, and information processing. There is plenty of room in the world of education for the pursuit of validation and verification of theories to broaden and question our knowledge. However, the lives of culturally and linguistically diverse students at risk should not be the currency of experimentation. Much like we know that penicillin will take care of strep throat, we also know which methods of teaching reading to CLDLs at risk are quantifiably validated. The research is clear about what works when teaching skilled reading to at-risk students. It is up to us as educators to do it.

We must implement with fidelity the methods and the sequences necessary for these children to learn on schedule and achieve standard benchmarks. There are three things that must be done.

First, begin with the basic foundation: language. The psycholinguistic theories mentioned on pages 33–36 are the underpinning for all comprehension at the early and later stages of reading development. Children who lack language also lack the schema required to make meaning of higher discourse. When examining your curricula, consider its implementation based upon levels of language theory and language and literacy theory at all grade levels. This will provide the requisite background knowledge needed to bring at-risk CLDLs to expected grade levels and to supplement the lack of academic language experienced in settings outside of the school.

Second, teach phonological awareness as a specific skill. Scientific studies support the need for phonological awareness, grapho-phonemic awareness, and phonics in the development of skilled reading. Studies that support a whole-language approach also recommend a balance of phonics instruction. Unfortunately, sometimes a lack of systematic curricula focusing on the explicit instruction of phonemic awareness and phonics leads teachers to ignore it as a component of instruction, basing the literacy block instead on independent and guided reading activities with little or no specific skill development (Frey et al. 2005). We must be very careful. Children's lives are at stake.

Finally, focus on reading fluency with accuracy to automaticity and prosody. There is a correlation between automaticity of reading and comprehension. In fact, higher levels of fluency and automaticity result in higher levels of comprehension restricted only by corresponding levels of aural, or receptive, language. While multiple repeated readings of decodable texts is beneficial, the text must be presented in multiple contexts to promote fluency and to decrease the possibility of loss of engagement.

Much work has been done with the passage of the Reading Excellence Act, the No Child Left Behind Act, Reading First, and the findings of the National Reading Panel. However, these programs focused on early literacy, impacting learning mostly in grades K–3. The core of reading, comprehension, reading in the content areas, and reading for secondary or higher education has been neglected. Unfortunately, the days when a high school diploma and third-grade literacy skills sufficed to provide a middle-class lifestyle are gone. Even the most menial of jobs requires higher literacy, often of a technical nature, and very often computer skills.

Secondary literacy provides a more challenging task to educators than does primary literacy. It also has bigger implications. Consider these sobering statistics:

- Approximately eight million young people between the fourth and twelfth grade struggle to read at grade level (U.S. Department of Education 2003).

- Some 70% of these older readers require some form of remediation (U.S. DOE 2003).

- Every school day, more than 3,000 students drop out of high school (Joftus and Maddox-Dolan 2003).

- Only 70% of high school students graduate on time with a regular diploma, and fewer than 60% of African-American and Latino students do so (Greene 2002).

- High school students in the lowest 25% of their class are 20 times more likely to drop out than the highest performing students.

- Approximately 53% of high school graduates enroll in remedial courses in post-secondary education (NCES 2003).

These statistics make us question the education our K–12 children are receiving. There are two reasons why ensuring adequate ongoing literacy development for all students in the middle and high school years is a more challenging task than ensuring excellent reading education in the primary grades. First, secondary school literacy skills are more complex, more embedded in subject matters, and more content specific. Second, adolescents are not as universally motivated to be better readers or as interested in school-based reading as they were when they were kindergarteners. We must not limit our RTI thinking to the lower grades—big kids need intervention, too.

The Pedagogical Spectrum

As we begin to examine instructional practices in use in our classrooms, we must also examine the curriculum as to its explicitness and systematic methodology. The pedagogical spectrum (see figure 2.11) may assist us with eliminating both *dysteachia* and soft bigotry by expanding our knowledge of what other methods exist and understanding just where our present practices lie. One method of intensive instruction that has been repeatedly validated with culturally and linguistically diverse learners at-risk is direct instruction (Engelmann 2006). Direct instruction is a methodology that many teachers approach with hesitation. Rather than recognizing that this method might be best for children, direct instruction is often dismissed as an infringement upon teacher expertise and creativity. We must remember it is student need— not teacher desire—that needs to drive instruction in the classroom. Once the results become apparent, most teachers find the passion for teaching at-risk learners that is shared with you in this book.

Fig. 2.11. The Pedagogical Spectrum

Theory to Practice

- Create a pedagogical spectrum for the curricula in place at your school at present. Use the model from figure 2.11 to help you.

- If you have some form of RTI in practice, or if you are developing your model, identify the tier at which each of the curricula is used.

- Share and discuss the spectrum and the rationale for placement of curricula with your colleagues.

Conclusion

The question of why culturally and linguistically diverse learners struggle in many of our schools is a sensitive one. There are two all-too-common practices that undermine and damage instructional practice: the soft bigotry of low expectations and dysteachia. Examining the basic structures of seven theories on the teaching of reading enables us to look at our own position on a pedagogical spectrum, and allows us to begin to build schema about our own beliefs and the knowledge we have yet to acquire.

Reflect and Act

1. Identify students in your class in need of Tier 2 and Tier 3 instruction. What is your preferred method of instruction? What are the theoretical underpinnings of this method? What quantitative, scientific evidence supports this method? After reading this chapter, will you make any adjustments?

2. What percentage of students are operating at or above grade-level proficiency on a (preferably) nationally-normed assessment? Of the one or two theories of instruction that most closely fits your teaching paradigm, describe the implications for students in need of Tier 2 and Tier 3 interventions.

3. Complete the Theory to Practice activity (page 42). Begin the discussion with your peers as suggested.

Chapter 3

Instruction or Intervention? Which "I" for RTI?

Your philosophy of teaching and learning drives your curriculum development, and the chosen curriculum drives instructional delivery. In this age of accountability, most curriculum centers on standards, which determine exactly what children must learn, in what sequence it should be taught, and to what level it must be mastered. Using the standards provides structure to both design and implementation, since there are specific measurements for outcomes to determine the effectiveness of the design and delivery. On the pedagogical spectrum illustrated in Chapter 2, a scientifically based, scientifically validated partnership of curriculum design and instructional delivery is optimum.

What is RTI? The Classroom Teacher as First Responder

It is important to look at RTI from the practitioner perspective. After all, the teacher is really the first responder when it comes to providing instructional rescue for students. We will take a good look at what RTI is in an objective, nonphilosophical sense and examine some models that may be familiar. Then, we will look at the minimum requirements for a solid RTI implementation. So first, just what does Response to Intervention, or RTI, mean? There are many definitions, but essentially, RTI means having a system that involves both core instruction and intervention using scientifically based, and preferably scientifically

Check Yourself

- What do I know about research-validated practices?
- What do I know about the needs of my students?
- Does my instruction match their needs?
- Am I monitoring the effectiveness of those strategies and practices?
- Are there any ineffective programs and strategies in place?

validated curriculum and pedagogical practices. RTI is about addressing student needs based on either a standard treatment protocol or a problem-solving approach to guide instructional practice. RTI requires frequent progress monitoring of student performance using a validated measuring instrument. Progress monitoring provides the quantitative data that is used to drive instructional decision-making. Before moving forward, we need a common understanding of all that terminology. Figure 3.1 shows a brief glossary of terms and their meanings.

Fig. 3.1. Glossary of Terms

Term	Definition
scientifically based	Curricula and practices that are founded on research. A good example would be getting the report of the National Reading Panel (2000) and implementing a curriculum that references the research found in the report.
scientifically validated	The gold standard of practices, and more importantly curricula, this term refers to methods that have been repeatedly proven using a scientific approach to work. A scientifically validated curriculum will have been tested and verified by third parties (not the publishers) to produce the outcomes they claim. For example, phonics is a scientifically validated practice, with specific sequences, levels of intensity, and levels of explicitness that vary depending on the curricula chosen.
standard-treatment protocol	A specific and consistent practice of providing an intervention, continually monitoring progress, examining data, and making adjustments to instruction based on the data.
problem-solving approach	Taking a holistic view of the instructional needs of students, and implementing a school-wide change to address overarching problems. Generally, RTI is an element of a school- or district-wide problem-solving approach to reduce special education referrals.
progress monitoring	The practice of assessing student performance and evaluating the effectiveness of instruction or intervention. Progress monitoring may use any number of instruments commercially available that have been scientifically validated.

With some common language, we can move on to what makes RTI work. For RTI to be most effective, it should be developed and implemented as a comprehensive system. Piecemeal and classroom-by-classroom approaches, although supportive for the students, do not address the larger issues that may arise in schools and districts, thus failing to solve the root problem it is intended to address.

If you answered "no" to two or more of the Check Yourself questions (at right), you need to enlist the assistance of one or more of your grade-level peers, or even consider a school-wide examination of RTI. While you are the first responder, you still need a team to respond to a larger crisis. In a comprehensive RTI implementation, instructional decisions are based on student performance data on one or more commonly determined assessments. The first thing to do is to adjust the lens through which we view our students. All general education students who may be paper-identified as a protected class—such as English language learners, mainstreamed special education, and Title I—are considered general education students first for the purpose of RTI. You might be surprised at the types of skill deficits that cross the student classes. Is an English language learner who struggles with phonemic awareness any different from an English-only student who struggles with the same issue? Often, the answer is no. When we put all the children into one group and use data to decide what needs must be addressed, we do a much more efficient and effective job of providing instruction than when we simply expose everyone to the same core and then make adjustments by classification.

In RTI, we use outcomes-based decision-making to provide the framework for any adjustments that are made, including the instructional approach; group size; intensity of intervention; time in intervention; and language development needs of students. This list is not comprehensive. For example, outcomes assessment may indicate that some teachers work better with a particular group, so the adjustment may involve assigning specific teachers to specific students or content areas.

RTI is a proactive approach to instruction. When designed and implemented with fidelity, RTI catches students as they begin to fall through the cracks of grade-level instruction, and before they experience prolonged academic failure.

You may need to conduct a needs assessment to examine the causes for CLDL underachievement in your school or classroom. A needs assessment should lead you to develop a targeted solution strategy that will allow the CLDL population to meet all benchmarks in the five essential components of reading: phonemic awareness, phonics, fluency, vocabulary, and comprehension (National Reading Panel 2000). Under the No Child Left Behind Act, there is an expectation that all students will read, write, and possess higher order thinking skills at grade level by the end of the third grade. As students are being assessed, we must consider those components of the assessment that measure comprehension separate from those that measure decoding skills. (This will be addressed in more detail later in relation to schema.) Culturally and linguistically diverse students, those who come from language backgrounds other than standard or academic English, tend not to meet early literacy skills. Typically, the needs of these students are addressed through professional development and curriculum adjustments. More often than not, these students require a paradigm shift in the way we do business in the classroom, the school, and the district.

Why is it that, in far too many classrooms, the instructional assistant, who does not have a teaching certificate, and sometimes not even a college degree, is expected to provide the differentiation for the struggling students? When you go to the doctor, does the physician only see the patients who are well, transferring the sick ones to the medical assistant?

Multiple Tiers, Multiple Models: One Comprehensive System

There is no single approach to RTI. RTI evolves, and hopefully in a way that maintains what's good as well as weeds out ineffective practices as they are uncovered. No matter the model or approach, four components are essential to any RTI framework and implementation, and these are often represented as four tiers of intervention:

- Tier 1: General instruction

- Tier 2: Targeted intervention

- Tier 3: Intensive intervention

- Tier 4: Special education

We will examine each tier in turn, although not in great depth. The four tiers are not new, nor are they unique to RTI, although they are essential to an effective implementation. Between 2000 and 2002, both California and Florida reading adoptions called for an alternative core program for students who were significantly below grade level as assessed at grades four and above. For more than 40 years, certain methodological approaches have relied on data-driven, multi-tiered, or differentiated instruction to address the needs of the various levels of students found in a single grade level. What is unique to RTI is the integration of the four tiers as a generally accepted, common practice in general education—something whole schools and districts can adopt regardless of their overall performance data.

The multi-tier model is often represented as a triangle (figure 3.2):

Fig. 3.2. The Multi-Tier Model

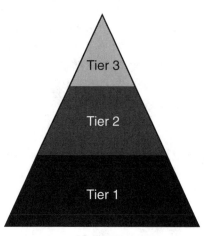

Based on our discussions, and the instructional practices outlined here, let's consider a model that looks more like figure 3.3:

Fig. 3.3. A New Model for General Education

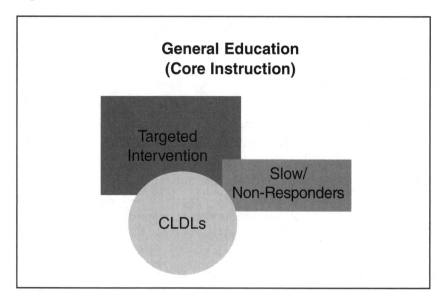

Notice the common terminology. Tier 1 is the general education, or core instruction; Tier 2 is targeted intervention; Tier 3 is intensive intervention. Neither figures show Tier 4, but where present, Tier 4 is generally a self-contained, special education setting. (Not all models include a fourth tier. Tier 4 is generally considered an alternate placement, such as a self-contained special education classroom.)

Tier 1

For Tier 1 to be preventative or proactive, the curriculum must address the needs of 85% of the students. This benchmark is now commonly agreed upon throughout the academic community. If the core instructional program does not maintain 85% of the students in a school or district at or above proficiency on multiple assessments, the school or district needs a stronger core. Many teachers feel that this 85% criterion is unreasonable, but in truth, most children should be proficient on multiple assessments. This may require a shift in mindset, particularly in chronically failing schools. Too often there is complacency and a resignation that the vast majority of our students will not be proficient or advanced. All that talk about raising expectations applies here.

As instructional time goes, 90–120 minutes of daily core, or Tier 1 instruction is common. When this time is reduced to less than 90 minutes, the number of students achieving proficiency decreases. Two hours is commonly required to address language arts in addition to reading instruction. Up to 150 minutes of core instruction may be implemented where higher risk factors such as high mobility, high poverty, and high concentrations of culturally and linguistically diverse learners are present. Keep in mind, these are daily numbers. Where an alternative scheduling model is in place (block, minimum day, etc.) it is important to keep those weekly instructional minutes in mind.

Rest assured that Tier 1 often presents the most problems because: 1) not enough instructional minutes are devoted to the core; 2) fidelity is not maintained, or 3) the wrong core is in place. If any one of these three situations exist in your classroom, you may find you need more intervention.

Tier 2

Tier 2 intervention has a higher degree of structure and intensity than Tier 1. In Tier 2, instruction is done in small groups, typically with 3–12 students who have a similar skill deficit. The key to effectiveness at this tier is *more*:

- more systematic
- more explicit
- more modeling
- more examples
- more scaffolding
- more feedback
- more opportunities

Tier 2 instruction and curricula must have more systematic instruction than the core instructional curricula. If your core reading program uses implicit phonics and your students are not meeting progress monitoring benchmarks, your Tier 2 curriculum must use *explicit* phonics. If your Tier 1 mathematics curriculum uses a reform approach and your children are not meeting progress monitoring benchmarks in basic fractions, your Tier 2 curriculum may need to move towards a *traditional* approach to fractions.

Tier 2 instruction and curricula must provide more modeling on the part of the instructor. There can be no assumptions made about students' background knowledge, or *schemata*. If a student in Tier 2 needs to say /*mmm*/ when he or she sees the letter *m*, then the teacher needs to model that skill. The teacher may need to provide one model, maybe three. It all depends on how quickly the student demonstrates mastery learning of the instruction being provided.

In Tier 2 instruction and curricula, the teacher must provide more examples and more scaffolding before calling upon students to produce independent responses. The teacher may need to say

/mmm/ three or four times; ask students to say /mmm/ chorally two times; and then finally ask one student to produce /mmm/ as a correct, independent response to the visual prompt of seeing the letter *m* in print.

In Tier 2 instruction and curricula, the teacher must provide more feedback. Moreover, that feedback must be both academically and behaviorally specific. Students must be told precisely what they are doing correctly, and be offered specific corrections when they err. In the case of the letter *m* example, if the teacher has modeled making the sound and provided guided practice, and yet the students produced /rrr/ instead of /mmm/ when shown the letter *m*, the teacher needs to provide the students (all of them, not just the students who erred) an academic correction. That correction might sound like this: "Listen everyone, that sound is /mmm/. Watch my mouth and listen: /mmm/. Now do it with me: /mmm/." Those students also need additional guided practice and a gradual removal of the scaffold.

To praise something that was done well, focus on behavior immediately following the error set and correction. Praise the students for using nice, strong voices. Praise them all for responding. The point is, praise them for something done right, and correct everything that is done wrong. (A more detailed discussion on praise and corrective feedback appears in Chapter 8.)

In Tier 2, instruction and curricula must provide every student with more opportunities to participate. In Tier 1 instruction, not all students necessarily provide individual responses during the course of instruction. In Tier 2, the expectation is that every student will participate, as this is a necessary element for monitoring progress and adjusting instruction at the moment a student experiences difficulty.

If attention to these seven areas were increased in your present classroom practice, it will go a good distance in helping to bring your students to the necessary benchmark. While you cannot change curricula overnight, you can beef up your instructional concepts and implement some of these practices.

How does this look in the classroom? Tier 2 instruction may occur among different groups of students within a classroom, and certainly across a grade level. Tier 2 groups need to be as homogeneous as possible. This is one of the reasons that school wide implementations of RTI are preferred. The student's homogeneous group is a determining factor in the pacing of instruction.

Finally, Tier 2 is about a treatment protocol for the student, not about force-fitting a piece of a core to use for remediation. Remember, if the core instruction is not meeting the needs of the student, it is time to examine their needs, not core offerings of remediation. (More about that when we get to the process of using data to inform instruction.)

Tier 3

Tier 3 intervention has a higher degree of structure and intensity than Tier 2. Tier 3 instruction is also done in small groups, typically with groups of 3–6 students of a very similar skill deficit. Students in Tier 3 are often two or more years below grade level, have suffered long-term failure, and may not have had consistent instruction or even access to education. These are students who need a very strong, focused intervention in order to bring them to grade level. For those reasons, think of Tier 3 instruction as an intensified version of Tier 2.

If the key to Tier 2 was *more*, the key to Tier 3 is *maximum*:

- maximum time
- maximum opportunities for practice and review
- maximum correction and feedback
- maximum engaged time on-task
- maximum repetition and practice review
- maximum breakdown of tasks into discrete, small steps
- maximum visibility of learning
- maximum prompting and cueing

For students who need Tier 3 intervention, exposure to the core may be a waste of their instructional time. That may sound controversial, but think of it in the following context: As a teacher, you have completed about 17 years of educational training. But suppose you were asked to take a class in a field where you had little to no experience, such as quantum physics? If you were required to be exposed to the grade-level curriculum, according to your grade level, you would be assigned to a post-doctoral course. Does this sound like nonsense? Yet this is precisely what happens when a sixth grade student who reads at a first grade level is placed into two hours of grade-level curriculum.

That's not to say that some children do not deserve academic enrichment through literature and problem solving and exploration. Of course they do! But these students must have the ability to read, write, think, calculate, and operate independently. They need to be able to graduate and move on to meaningful productive pursuits in their adult lives. To get there, they must be brought to grade level and kept there. Sometimes, that may involve some time away from the core so that the essential (i.e., basic) skills can be mastered. Not just taught—mastered!

So, in Tier 3 we supplant the core with instruction that is of the appropriate level and intensity to bring the student to grade level within two years. For example, instead of two hours in core and 30 minutes in intervention, the students get two-and-a-half hours in Tier 3 core intervention. This means an intervention program (often a curriculum) that provides comprehensive instruction at an accelerated pace to bring students to grade level very quickly.

The smaller group size and extended time in intervention allows students maximum opportunities for practice and review. Smaller groups offer more opportunities to hear from every student. Choral reading for decoding fluency takes on a new focus when each student reads every day. Small groups also facilitate the maximum opportunity for correction and feedback. Just as discussed previously in Tier 2, students cannot be left to err unchecked in Tier 3. A smaller group and increased focus on feedback and praise improves behavior, and students maximize their engaged time on task. Furthermore, if every student is experiencing success instead of frustration, behavioral problems are also reduced, and more time can be spent on-task. Finally, just like in Tier 2, a small group facilitates maximum repetition of newly introduced concepts, plus maximum practiced review of previously learned materials.

Just as in Tier 2, where children may struggle from a single skill deficit or be slightly below grade level, in Tier 3, no assumptions may be made about a student's ability to pick up a skill. Tasks are broken down into very small steps, with a focus on each individual skill required to build to the next skill set.

Here's a simplistic example. What skills are necessary for a child to read the words *cat, net, kit, cot,* and *cut?* He or she needs phonemic awareness, phoneme-grapheme correspondence, blending, and left-to-right sequencing. When we teach the words in isolation or in word families that do not provide the explicit strategy instruction for word attack and reading fluency, we risk having third-grade students who cannot make the transition from learning to read to reading to learn.

For at-risk students (and students in Tier 3 are definitely at-risk), learning needs to be visible and tangible. For students who are slow responders, additional prompts and cues assist in training the brain, creating the neuropathways that may be weak or absent, but are essential to performing reading and mathematics tasks with fluency and automaticity.

To teach the word *cat,* students need to know these three phonemes: /k/, /ă/, and /t/. Once they know the sounds, they must map those sounds to letters (phoneme-grapheme correspondence). The sound /k/ has multiple representations in print. Even though they need to know to use *c* when spelling *cat,* they should not generalize that *c* followed by any vowel makes the /k/ sound. It is vital that the teaching is explicit, visual, and clear.

Next, students need to be able to blend those three sounds together and produce a word. In English, blending requires moving from left-to-right in a word, so that sequence needs to be modeled by the teacher, perhaps by sliding his or her finger underneath the letters as the word is spoken. The teacher must provide models, guided practice, scaffolds, corrections, and multiple opportunities for independent practice. That sounds like a lot of work, but this is the level of explicitness required for students at Tier 3. Errors must be caught and corrected right away for students to glean accurate information and skills. They must stay on schedule in their learning, and to be able to consistently build new knowledge on appropriate schema. Tier 3 gives students the background, foundational knowledge upon which new knowledge is built.

Examining Commonalities of Tiers 2 and 3

The differences between Tier 2 and Tier 3 are shown below (figure 3.4), with recommended time frames for each provided.

Fig. 3.4. Tier 2 Versus Tier 3 Intervention

Element	Tier 2	Tier 3
Amount of daily instruction	30 minutes (in addition to Tier 1)	150 minutes (supplants Tiers 1 and 2)
Level of instruction	• slightly below grade level • single skill deficit	• significantly below grade level • multiple skill deficits
Duration	based on assessment	based on assessment
Group composition	• homogeneous • 1:3 to 1:12	• homogeneous • 1:3 to 1:6
Progress monitoring	every two weeks	every one to two weeks

Tiers 2 and 3 require daily instruction. Although many models suggest that Tier 2 instruction need not be offered daily, intervention effectiveness diminishes when students have less than daily exposure to the instruction. Tier 2 is in addition to core instruction, but Tier 3 is designed to supplant the core instruction.

Students in Tier 3 may be so far below grade level that they derive little to no benefit from exposure to the core.

The duration of any intervention is based on assessment with the intent to bring students to a level just above the core so that the reduction of support does not have such a great impact on student progress. (Assessment will be covered in detail in Chapter 4.)

Both tiers are effective only if the groups are homogeneous. Group sizes are determined by the curriculum recommendations—however, all intervention groups are small and homogeneous. (Research indicates better outcomes for groups of three as compared to students working individually.)

Progress monitoring is frequent with an interval of no more than two weeks in either tier. One week is generally preferred for Tier 3. (Progress monitoring is another topic detailed in Chapter 4.)

Fig. 3.5. RTI Flowchart

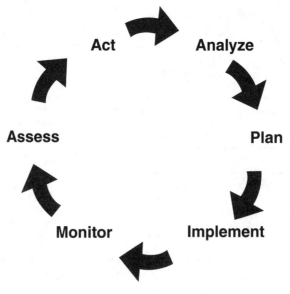

Round and Round

Armed with an understanding of the interventions tiers, how do they begin to work over the course of an instructional year? The next component of an RTI model is a method of problem solving. Figure 3.5 (previous page) shows the flow of an RTI model.

RTI is best understood as a constant round of six actions by the teacher: analyze, plan, implement, monitor, assess, and act. The process can begin at any of those points, but analysis is the best place to begin. The cycle is perpetual.

Analyze

In order to analyze student data, we must look at the present outcomes based on standardized test scores, curriculum-based assessments, and any other quantitative data the school has available. It is best to review at least three quantifiable assessments. For example, the core instruction may have an assessment that tells you how well the child is doing in the core. This may be expressed as a percentile, or a status (benchmark, proficient, etc.). Next, look at a standardized assessment, such as a state assessment or a nationally normed commercial assessment. Finally, an indicator of risk or screening device is an excellent and necessary tool for determining risk.

With data from three assessments, it is likely to have a match on risk for at least two out of the three. One word of caution: If your core instruction identifies a student as at or above proficient, but the risk indicator and the standardized assessment indicate a risk, look for a fourth marker. Since the curriculum-based measure only measures the mastery of the curriculum, you could have a mismatch between curriculum expectations and state standards of proficiency.

Plan

Now that you have information about where your students are, ask yourself, "Where should my students be?" How you answer that question will help you develop a plan for instruction that considers student needs, and necessary outcomes, as well as present and needed resources.

Implement

Once your plan is developed, you can move forward to put it in place. Implementation of an RTI plan is the most intense step in the process, and may take anywhere from three months to three years, depending on the scope of the plan. Some schools and districts that decide in June to implement RTI in the fall do not have a school- or district-wide model in place until August. Other schools decide that a cautious, phased-in rollout is the better option, and may take up to three years to bring this model to full implementation. However long it takes to implement, the next step is to monitor the plan. (See Chapter 9 for details on developing your implementation plan.)

Monitor

Monitoring is done on several levels. First, monitor for effectiveness of instruction. Is the instructional program meeting the needs of the students? Use a weekly, biweekly, or monthly, scientifically validated monitoring instrument. Also, monitor the appropriateness of the groupings. Are the groups receiving the attention they need? Are the groups too small? Too large? Is one student slowing the instructional pace? Does one student in the group need to move faster? Are there discipline problems in the group that could be alleviated by regrouping, by more appropriate instruction, or a different instructor? In short, ask questions! Ask lots of them as you seek to find the best possible fit for your students.

Assess

The next step is assessment. Assessment is made for student achievement and for fidelity of instruction based on direct observation and the work of professional learning communities. It is important to note that instructor assessment is a piece of this pie, as well. In a professional learning community we have to ask ourselves and our peers whether we are doing the best possible job of teaching our children. Are we meeting their needs or simply satisfying our own desires and philosophical bents? It is a tough task to examine our practices, as well as those of our peers, but it is a task that must be assumed if we are to implement a change in practice that improves both teaching and learning.

Act

With all of this information in hand, it is time to act. Decide, based on the data, whether to regroup students, reassign support teachers, move students between tiers (up or down), or provide professional development. Once these adjustments have been made, return to the beginning of the cycle by analyzing what did and did not work, modifying the plan, and so on.

Whether a standard treatment protocol or other method is employed often depends on the curriculum that is implemented. Some curricula are better suited to a standard treatment protocol while others may be better suited to a looser, or more qualitative method of decision-making. Deciding on a standard treatment protocol is easier after understanding assessment.

Conclusion

This chapter examined RTI from the practitioner's perspective. The teacher is the first responder in the instructional rescue of students. Wrapping your mind around RTI takes some time, but it is important to understand it. This chapter touched upon some examples of models that you may have seen and provided the minimum requirements for a solid RTI implementation.

Reflect and Act

Perform a needs analysis of your CA-RTI implementation. Use these questions as the starting point for a more comprehensive analysis to be completed for a larger implementation.

1. Analyze your core curriculum as outlined on pages 50–52.

2. What percentage of your students are not meeting proficiency benchmarks in reading? What percentage of culturally and linguistically diverse learners are not meeting these benchmarks?

3. Gather data on students (either this year's, if available, or last year's) using three to four different assessments. Are there variances in achievement levels in the multiple assessments? (For example, does one assessment indicate 93% of students are proficient while another indicates only 62% are proficient on the same type of skills?) If students have varying levels of proficiency across assessments, work will need to be done to determine which data is valid.

Chapter 4

Screen for Problems and Monitor Progress

Assessing Assessment

Chapter 3 examined RTI from the practitioner's perspective and offered a good working definition of RTI, and perhaps revealed some elements that are already at work in your classroom or school. Now it's time to take a look at assessment, which is a necessary tool for establishing goals, driving instruction, and examining the effectiveness of our practices. Our culture is riddled with testing and prepping, often without much thought as to why, what is being measured, and whether or not the best tool for the job is being utilized.

Practitioner's Perspective

I remember reading in my graduate studies that assessment served many purposes. My perspective on assessment has changed over the years. As an undergraduate I thought it was simply designed to thin the ranks of the weak, faint of heart, or those majoring in partying. Now I look more toward researchers, such as Hlebowitsh (2005), who wrote, "To put it simply, assessment is designed to show what a person knows or can do."

Check Yourself

- What screening assessments are you using and for what purpose?

- What diagnostic assessments are you using and for what purpose?

- What progress monitoring tools are you using and for what purpose?

- What outcomes-based assessments are you using and for what purpose?

Whether in written, oral, formal, informal, or anecdotal forms, assessment should drive instruction. It helps teachers determine not only what students have learned but what has not been effectively taught. Assessment may be used to determine a baseline, showing where students are when they enter the classroom. Assessment provides data used to develop remediation, intervention, or enrichment instruction. As such, it is an integral part of the CA-RTI model. In the CA-RTI model, a valid assessment used at specific intervals determines whether or not a chosen instructional method is appropriate to close the achievement gap and erase an indication of risk for a student. Multiple data points provide feedback that informs the teacher about student progress—and, more specifically, identifies specific skill deficits.

Make a list of all the tests, screens, and progress monitors in use in your classroom. Use the Assessment Matrix (figure 4.1) on page 65 to help you. We will revisit these at the end of the chapter when you should have a much better idea as to whether or not you are on assessment overload; don't have enough tools; or are using a hammer when a screwdriver is the better tool for the job.

Fig. 4.1. Assessment Matrix

Assessment Type	Name	Purpose	Frequency	Does it provide actionable data?
(Ex:) Screen	Beginning Reading Inventory	Determine level of risk based on reading skills	Four times/year	Yes

An Instinctive Response

For some, the word assessment is equated with the word test, which can cause a negative physiological reaction. The negative connotation is difficult to shake. However, in teaching and learning, one must realize that assessment remains the only standard yardstick with which to measure success.

Practitioner's Perspective

At a pivotal juncture in my teaching career, I went from teaching high school social sciences to teaching sixth grade multiple subjects in a self-contained classroom. A federal housing project provided the homes for the vast majority of the students. Many elements influenced this assignment change, not the least of which was a desire to work with at-risk youth. I quickly found that the standard "best practices" I learned in college were inadequate to teach these sixth graders to read. Most of them operated at approximately the second grade level. After implementing a rigorous scientifically-based, research-validated curriculum designed to accelerate older struggling readers for most of one year, I could see the difference in my students. However, state test scores and our academic performance index rating would be the greater determinant of our success. The sixth grade teaching team had spent the year focused solely on reading, knowing that if our students could at least read the test, they stood a greater chance of performing better across all subjects. The gamble paid off. The teaching team simply told its students to do what they did every day in class; use the strategies teachers had been teaching them, and do their best. Beyond that, nothing more could be asked. When the principal reported the results, the team was shocked to hear that, for the first time in more than 10 years, sixth grade showed an increase in average stanine and percentile over fifth grade. The following years saw the implementation expand to other grade levels and resulted in a rise in test scores. The assessment judged our performances as teachers, not the students' abilities as learners.

The Basics of Assessment in CA-RTI

There are two reasons to keep tabs on assessments. The first reason is to determine what to teach. The second is to determine how to teach it. Whether for initial placement and directionality, pace and acceleration, or grouping and regrouping, the measurements should be seen as tools to help bring students to benchmark as quickly and appropriately as possible, and then never let them fail. Many factors influence student performance. We have all read or been lectured on teacher ability and expectations. Raise the bar, and the students will follow. But how high should we raise it? When should we lower it? How long do we leave it at each level?

Assessment helps answer those questions, or rather, drives the instruction. While standards-based assessments are preferred in the CA-RTI model, that preference is predicated on the establishment of standards that are normative across demographics and common to all states. As the majority of states have adopted the Common Core Curriculum Standards, expect assessments to change to reflect that trend.

While using assessment to drive instruction is ideal every year, this is often a reactive model. Ideally, a proactive use of assessment data would involve analyzing the trend data (what is seen from year to year), and adjusting Tier 1 instruction so that fewer students fall into Tier 2. Measurement of growth and fidelity of implementation should also be analyzed to determine effectiveness of instructional delivery.

Choose wisely when analyzing your present assessments, or shopping for new ones. Very few provide consistent information clearly reflected by observations of classroom practices. Some screening devices do contain comprehensive reporting and evaluative tools. However, those tools often require a subscription to their services. The best assessments do not rely on state standards for development of content. They rely on the valid science that predicts reading failure or success based on norms from a large and diverse demographic. Make sure that your students are represented in those norms.

In addition, the best assessments not only measure student success, but are predictive in the future accomplishments of students. Examining only grade equivalents, scaled scores, percentiles, and stanines of multiple-normed assessments may paint a murkier picture of the ability and progress of students than if examining growth on a standardized growth-modeled indicator of risk.

You Make the Diagnosis

To understand the importance of assessment in a CA-RTI implementation, examine the basis for your RTI goals. An abundance of literature exists on the importance of scientifically-based, reading-researched instruction in the primary grades. Snow's extensive works document the most commonly cited cause for retention in the primary grades as the inability to meet grade-level benchmarks in reading (Beswick, Willms, and Sloat 2005). Also, reading difficulties know no bounds of ethnicity, socioeconomic strata, or linguistic diversity. Children who are poor readers in the primary grades rarely, if ever, catch up.

Struggling with Reading Is Persistent and Pervasive

There does not seem to be any consensus along the lines of a single measure or type of assessment providing a solitary best practice for assessing literacy instruction. However, a bit of a *détente* does exist to support well-standardized measures (Beswick, Willms, and Sloat 2005; Kame'enui et al. 2006). Consider the appropriate use of the tools. Construct validity, the extent to which the results of an assessment clearly indicates the skill levels intended to be measured, is frequently compromised when assessment misuse occurs. This happens frequently when educators attempt to use a screening measure to place students in groups. Another frequent compromise of construct validity occurs with measures designed to assign English language learners to English language development (ELD) levels and create sheltered classrooms based on the assessment. (See Chapter 7.) Researchers also agree and recommend using a variety of assessments, each with a specific purpose, for greater validity than a solitary measure. This lends support to the CA-RTI model's suggested practice of using multiple assessments. Most teachers do not like to take time away from instruction to test or assess. Unfortunately, without taking the time to assess, how do we know what is working, what is not working, and what we need to do to fix it? If instruction is the medicine, assessment is the lab work that indicates drug and dosage. Many commercially published assessment measures have high levels of construct validity, and teacher bias in determining student performance has been shown to decrease with the use of standardized assessments (Beswick, Willms, and Sloat 2005).

Four Measurements

There are really four types of assessment that are critical to RTI implementation: screening, diagnostic, progress monitoring, and outcomes-based (Kame'enui et al. 2006). (A fifth assessment, subgroup identification assessments, most frequently determines the language development level of students whose home language surveys indicate that a language other than English may be used in the home. See Chapter 7 for a detailed discussion.) These four measurements (figure 4.2) work in a continuous loop to provide educators guidance and feedback as to the effectiveness of instruction for all children.

Fig. 4.2. Assessment Loop

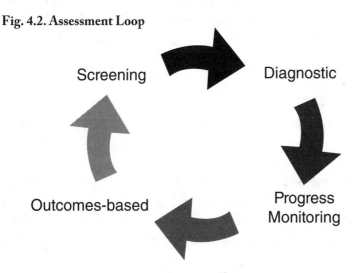

Screening

The purpose of a screening device is to determine whether or not children are in need of support. Screening measures simply determine baseline levels of indicated risk of reading failure. Early screening tools at grades K–3 are generally designed to determine whether or not a risk of failure exists. Screens are not diagnostic, even if they have been used that way. They are not all designed to place students into an instructional program, pace, or level. Imagine checking your blood pressure at the grocery store after aerobics class, and determining that you need medication because of the elevated pressure. That is just as inappropriate! Too often, being designated as an English language learner or qualifying for free and reduced lunch are the most widely used screens for determining whether or not a student might need instructional support. Just as being a certain ethnicity does not make a person more or less likely to have osteoporosis, it is too broad an assumption that if a child is exposed to a language other than English at home, that he or she will need additional support in order to enjoy academic success in the English-speaking classroom. There is also an assumption that a child living in poverty will need additional support or intervention in order to enjoy academic success. For these children, screening devices are employed early on because their life circumstances make them more likely to be at risk.

Most screening devices designate a child as being at little or no risk of failure, some risk of failure, or great risk of failure. Various devices use terms such as *benchmark, proficient, advanced, strategic,* and *intensive.* The exact meaning of each of those terms depends on the population against whom the screening device is normed, and the cultural and linguistic diversity of the child.

Think of the screening device as the triage phase of intervention. It simply tells the level of care needed by the student. Bear in mind, even the most conscientious triage unit is not omniscient. Some symptoms of risk may be masked. Consider a child who may have spent hours playing with alphabet tiles before beginning kindergarten and may be fairly proficient at rapid letter naming but has absolutely no phonemic or phonological awareness.

Without screening across several beginning reading skills, it is possible to miss providing the instruction that is necessary to get to and maintain proficiency. Evaluating the data can assist in determining the effectiveness of the core curriculum in preventing or eliminating designations of risk. If grade-level students who only participate in Tier 1 instruction have declining scores in the screening assessment, indicating that risk increases as the year progresses, it is time to shop for a new Tier 1 curricula.

Screening measurements should be taken at three or four data points during the instructional year. Frequency of assessment varies as indicated by performance measure, assessment design, and implementation fidelity. At a minimum, Tier 1 students should be screened three times each year: within the first 30 days of instruction; at mid-year; and within the last 30 days of instruction. For students at Tiers 2 and 3, four times each year is preferred. The four intervals are based on a 180-instructional-day calendar. For at-risk students, an earlier start to intervention means more ground gained during the year. The initial screen should take place within the first 10 days of instruction so that intervention may begin immediately, if not sooner.

The calendar in figure 4.3 below shows a suggested time line for screening.

Fig. 4.3. Screening Time Line

	Initial	Mid-Year 1	Mid-Year 2	End-of-Year
Day of Instruction	1–10	30–40	90–100	150–170

Start with a screen for all students. For those who have an indication of risk, diagnose where the risk lies. In addition, rely on other measurements, particularly continuous progress monitoring, to make certain that you are not withholding appropriate instruction to students who may have been overlooked during the initial screening.

Diagnostic

The sole purpose of a diagnostic assessment is to examine all of the presenting symptoms. Analyze the symptoms, come up with a finding, and identify exactly what skill or skill level is appropriate for beginning intervention. The diagnostic assessment serves to validate the need for instructional support. It may guide classroom instruction and support. At times, depending on your choice of curriculum, an in-program diagnostic serves as a placement tool for determining the entry level and pace of instruction that is appropriate for the student.

For students whose screening clearly indicates only a single skill deficit, it might be enough to provide skill-specific instruction—but how do you make that determination? If a third-grade student's test indicates a deficit in fluency, is it because he or she is a slow reader? Is the student language deficient? Does the student have limited sight-word recognition? Poor phonics? Some intervention programs contain both diagnostic assessments and placement tests. These are often trustworthy for program placement. Some even contain screening devices and correlations to multiple screening and diagnostic assessments to assist you in placing your students. If you are using a third-party assessment, it should direct you to specific or multiple skills and instructional levels for intervention.

Progress Monitoring

The progress monitor is a tool to check the vitals. It measures a skill and checks it against a norm. It allows you to look at a trajectory of growth from one check to the next. Sometimes it will indicate no growth or even a decline. This information is used to adjust instruction. The frequency of progress monitoring depends on the level of intensity, or tier, of instruction.

For students in Tier 3, progress monitoring of some sort should be done weekly. For students in Tier 2, every one to two weeks may suffice. (*Note:* If you are using these intervals as a guide, make sure that your school's designation of tiers is consistent with the definitions provided here. One school's Tier 4 is another's Tier 2. The labels do not matter as much as the indication of risk. With adolescent learners, daily progress monitoring using fluency benchmarks is becoming commonplace. While it is not recommended that you spend an hour each day listening to every one of your middle school intervention students read a fluency passage, it is quite feasible to have students assess each other. However, I would strongly recommend that a certificated teacher monitor that peer assessment, listening to two or three students each day to help guide them.)

The progress-monitoring tool you use can help to determine student progress toward benchmarks and/or between benchmarks. Your progress-monitoring tool should guide your daily classroom instruction and support. If students are not quite meeting benchmarks, increase the intensity. If they are well ahead of a benchmark, consider skipping lessons or accelerating instruction. If students are flatlining or worse, declining, it might be time to change the curriculum.

Use the calendar in figure 4.4 (on the next page) to help plan for appropriate screening and progress monitoring intervals throughout the year.

Fig. 4.4. Progress Monitoring Intervals

Week	Term	All Students	Tier 1 Students	Tier 2/Tier 3 Students
1	1st Quarter	beginning-of-year screen		
2				
3		begin intervention		progress monitor
4				progress monitor
5				progress monitor
6				progress monitor and regroup
7				progress monitor
8			progress monitor Tier 2 redesignees	progress monitor

Fig. 4.4. Progress Monitoring Intervals *(cont.)*

Week	Term	All Students	Tier 1 Students	Tier 2/Tier 3 Students
9	2nd Quarter			progress monitor
10	2nd Quarter	first mid-year screen (if four times/year)	regroup based on mid-year screen results	progress monitor
11	2nd Quarter			progress monitor
12	2nd Quarter		progress monitor Tier 2 redesignees	progress monitor
13	2nd Quarter			progress monitor
14	2nd Quarter	mid-year screen (if three times/year)	regroup based on mid-year screen results	progress monitor and regroup
15	2nd Quarter			progress monitor
16	2nd Quarter		progress monitor Tier 2 redesignees	progress monitor
17	3rd Quarter			progress monitor
18	3rd Quarter		progress monitor Tier 2 redesignees	progress monitor
19	3rd Quarter			progress monitor
20	3rd Quarter		progress monitor Tier 2 redesignees	progress monitor
21	3rd Quarter			progress monitor
22	3rd Quarter	second mid-year screen (if four times/year)	Regroup based on mid-year screen results	progress monitor and regroup
23	3rd Quarter			progress monitor
24	3rd Quarter			progress monitor
25	4th Quarter		progress monitor Tier 2 redesignees	progress monitor
26	4th Quarter			progress monitor
27	4th Quarter		progress monitor Tier 2 redesignees	progress monitor
28	4th Quarter			progress monitor
29	4th Quarter	end-of-year screen	make recommendations for next year's placement	progress monitor
30	4th Quarter			progress monitor
31	4th Quarter			make recommendation for referral to study team or next year's placement

Outcomes Based Assessments

Outcomes-based assessments are designed to measure significant gains or losses in student performance. Because of variances of purpose and intensities of intervention, the intervals vary depending on the tool. Outcomes-based measures may be in-program assessments that are administered at specific intervals. Most commonly, we think of the unit assessments in commercial curricula as outcomes-based, curriculum-based assessments. You may also administer a third-party, outcomes-based measure. The high-stakes assessments that are administered annually at some or all grade levels are outcomes-based, as well. For the purpose of a CA-RTI implementation, and as a tool to drive instruction, this book only focuses on the assessments that provide clear and immediate feedback about instruction and student progress. There is not much you can do about adjusting instruction based on last year's high-stakes assessment when the data received in September reflects the progress of the students from the previous school year. That doesn't mean the data is irrelevant or should be disregarded, but it is important to stick to what is under your immediate control.

Curriculum Based, Outcomes Based Measurement

Depending on the chosen curriculum, your curriculum-based outcomes-based measurement may or may not be designed to assist you in providing remedies for failed points on the assessments. Think about the curriculum-based outcomes-based measurements you have in your toolbox and determine whether they can truly guide instruction or if they simply serve as a snapshot. Strong curriculum-based outcomes-based measurements will provide enough detailed information for you to address the weaknesses students showed on the assessment, and then you can craft a meaningful lesson before continuing with instruction. If you have that capability, take full advantage of it. (I call these "guided curriculum-based outcomes-based measurements," which makes them sound like missiles—in a sense, they are weapons, and necessary to your arsenal of assessment tools.)

If your curriculum-based outcomes-based measurements is not of the guided variety, think about the other ways you can make use of the data it offers. As a rule of thumb, remember—if 85% of the students did not score at 85% or higher, then either the curriculum or the instruction was flawed. There is nothing wrong with the students, only the tools we use to serve them. Assessment is as much about us and the choices we make as teachers. Use the curriculum-based outcomes-based measurements as a reflective tool for your teaching as well as student learning.

The Roles of Assessment, Data, and AYP

All tools have a purpose and data provides information to help us, not hurt us. Data is our friend. District adequate yearly performance (AYP) goals are generally based on the performance of students on commercially published standardized tests and state or nationally-normed tests.

Practitioner's Perspective

We spend a great deal of time and energy analyzing the results of our state high-stakes testing.

"...assessing our students yearly with statewide tests [does not provide] enough data for us to determine whether or not they are achieving—just as knowing only a marathon runner's finish time would not convey enough information to understand and predict his current or future success. These test results are also inadequate to provide all of the information necessary to ascertain if we are educating all of our students well, or helping them succeed. Only a systemic approach to information will provide the appropriate solution (Golden 2005)."

State-normed assessments are frequently normed down for a rosier picture of student achievement than nationally-normed assessments.

Teacher Observation as Assessment: Protocol or Pitfall?

Teachers must sometimes be cautioned to avoid testing students whose siblings were prior students, since there is sometimes an unconscious bias towards that student. Research suggests the greatest improvement in assessment reliability and validity might be seen by eliminating teacher observation as the most prevalent form of assessment in the early grades. Here's why: Teacher observation has limited evidence of validity. Only 14% of teacher observations have good reliability data. Even less than that show evidence of concurrent or predictive validity (Beswick, Willms, and Sloat 2005).

Moreover, teacher observation is subject to cultural discrepancies, perceptions, expectations, and other extraneous factors that result in the overrepresentation of culturally and linguistically diverse learners in special education classes (Abedi 2004; Beswick, Willms, and Sloat 2005; Chamberlain 2005; Tivnan and Hemphill 2005). Err on the side of caution. Although we would all like to think we have no prejudices, we are human. There are enough valid assessments that do not rely solely on subjective teacher observations.

This is not to underplay the value of observation and teacher instinct and the teacher-student relationship built between teacher and student. These factors can and should influence instructional decisions, or at the very least, lead the teacher to begin an investigation using scientifically-validated measurements. Use one of those to justify intervention.

Get Tech Savvy

If you have the ability, technology helps. Modern devices have made assessment much more precise. With technology, assessment results may be more quickly analyzed so that you may adjust instruction. But before you turn all of your assessment needs over to a computer, keep in mind that the human element in assessment cannot be ignored. True, certain assessment results will be more precise and more quickly returned. Technology may also help drive your remediation activities (especially if the remediation activities are written by the same publisher). But your expertise as the experienced teacher will be vital for determining whether your student is encountering difficulties because of a cultural or linguistic diversity issue—and technology cannot account for that. New equipment may be pricey up front, but it can save you both time and money over the long haul. Based on the results of a pilot program in 100 Texas schools during the 2002–2003 school year, a large elementary school expected to save, on average, 150 instructional hours—or four weeks of instructional time—by using screening and progress monitoring software rather than traditional paper-based methods (Berry 2006).

Spaced repetition is good for mastery learning. Not all assessment is valid. That which is valid, however, must be used to direct our teaching and improve student learning. As I travel from state to state, I see numerous differences in the quality and quantity of assessment that takes place in our schools. While state standards are clearly defined, including curriculum frameworks, program design and implementation remain murky. This is why there is such a need for multiple assessments.

Perhaps through this discussion you find that your depth of knowledge on the finer points of assessment could use some professional development. Commonly, schools find a need to increase their awareness on the construct validity of assessments used at their sites. Put this on your professional development "to do" list. Teachers must be able to work with a solid understanding of the purposes and constraints of the assessment tools mandated or at their disposal. Most practitioners can benefit from additional professional development on the bias inherent in assessment delivery when cultural differences between students and teachers result in over-referral of CLDLs for special education services.

Practitioner's Perspective

I firmly believe that assessment remains one of the most valuable tools in teaching and learning. Without assessment, we do not know what we have taught to retention. Without baseline assessment, we do not know our students' skills when they come to us. Without informal assessment during teaching, we cannot adjust instruction to ensure concept development or comprehension. Without normed assessments, we cannot determine whether or not learning progresses at an appropriate rate. How will we know whether or not we have equipped our children with the tools and skills necessary to compete in a global economy if we do not assess?

Conclusion

To use a construction metaphor, consider that all teachers are builders. Some build mansions, while others do not set their sights quite so high. These diverse buildings are being constructed right next door to one another, and all from the same raw materials. Some are built to code; some far surpass the code; others do not even meet minimum safety requirements.

Assessment is like a uniform building code. It can help to measure the creation of a uniform foundation for the teaching of literacy skills. Standards-based assessments provide a framework for measuring growth and achievement for all children in all classrooms based on the science of teaching reading and developmental measures at specific data-points in the K–12 continuum. This data should impact our delivery of instruction in clear and measurable ways.

Reflect and Act

Take a moment now to reflect on the questions offered at the beginning of this chapter:

- What screening assessments are you using and what is the purpose of each?

- What diagnostic assessments are you using and what is the purpose of each?

- What progress monitoring tools are you using and what is the purpose of each?

- What outcomes-based assessments are you using and what is the purpose of each?

Untangle the assessment web that often entangles schools and classrooms. Use the matrix in figure 4.1 to help you address the following questions. Work with a colleague and share your findings.

1. What does this information imply about your school's assessment practices? What steps will you need to take?

2. Do you have the right tools? Are you using a hammer when a screwdriver is the better tool for the job?

Chapter 5

The Importance of a Strong Core Program

There are three considerations for planning instruction: curriculum, instruction, and student needs. These elements essentially represent what to teach, how to teach it, and how to determine who is learning it effectively. This chapter defines and provides an overview of each of the three considerations, a model framework for implementation, and guiding questions for making decisions about curriculum and instruction driven by the needs of the students. The most comprehensive approach to organizing and planning instruction within these three domains is a Response to Intervention (RTI) (Stecker, Fuchs, and Fuchs 2005).

The basic components of literacy connect like the bones of a skeleton. But what happens when one of the bones is not fully developed? Use phonemic awareness as an example. Phonemic awareness is a critical building block of literacy. It is also a block that, if not properly formed, hinders the development of literacy into adolescence for some struggling readers. We hear the term all the time, but what is phonemic awareness? It consists of four components: rhyme, syllabication, blending, and segmenting. If you teach older students, think about whether or not they can syllabicate. Can they blend and segment words by phonemes, not syllables? Does low fluency in an older struggling reader connect to a primary skill like phonemic awareness? The answers are, "yes!"

Another common term is *scope and sequence*. What does it mean? Spiraling and scaffolding are not appropriate scope and sequence. This is particularly true for students who are the target of intervention instruction. Scope and sequence are critical elements of teaching early literacy skills to CLDLs at risk. *Scope* refers to the breadth and horizontal coverage of a discrete skill or set of skills over time; *sequence* refers to the vertical alignment, the step-by-step process of introducing new skills or subcomponents of a skill.

In your core instruction, it is critical that scope and sequence be appropriately aligned over the course of the year. This makes the "creation" of a core curriculum by individual classroom teachers particularly problematic. Scope and sequence of instruction must be articulated from one grade level to the next. If the articulation is not accurate, the scope is not broad enough, or the sequence is not logical enough as students move from grade to grade or from room to room, some students will get lost. If teachers stray too far from the articulated scope and sequence, even in the name of creativity—well-intended as this may be—they could be creating holes in students' instruction that will later result in students who are unable to reach benchmarks of proficiency on screening devices. This leads to the next two concerns when examining the core: curriculum and instruction.

For the purpose of this CA-RTI model, *curriculum* is defined as the general and specific concepts, skills, and content that is developed and delivered with fidelity through instruction to transmit the core skills, knowledge, and thought processes required of students to become productive members of the society in which they will choose to live. Curriculum is that component of schooling that serves as the foundation of instruction; that which may be planned, enacted, and experienced with scientific protocols, and its efficacy measured through qualitative, formative, as well as quantitative summative assessments that are valid and reliable for the population being assessed. That's a weighty definition. Read it again. Think about it.

This definition may seem somewhat esoteric and far from succinct. However, we must look at curriculum as the means of prescribing help. Therefore, design, implementation, monitoring, and assessment all fall under the umbrella of curriculum. In other words, you cannot separate what you teach from how you teach it and assess it. You cannot separate the culture of self from the implementation of the curriculum materials purchased for your classroom.

Instruction is a subset of curriculum. It is what happens in the classroom when teachers and students interact and bring the curriculum to life. Instruction incorporates the strategies teachers use to deliver the curriculum, and includes how the curriculum is taught: small group, whole class, homogeneous groups, heterogeneous groups, flexible groups, or cooperative groups. Instruction includes the fidelity to the explicitness or implicitness of the curriculum.

Instruction and curriculum are inexorably intertwined. (See figure 5.1.) Response to intervention is driven by the needs of the students. If RTI is seen as a system that involves both core instruction and scientifically-based and scientifically validated curriculum, then intervention will address student needs based on either a standard treatment protocol or a problem-solving approach to guide instructional practice.

RTI requires frequent monitoring of student performance using a validated measuring instrument. This provides the quantitative data to drive instructional decision making. This model begins with all students in the general education population.

Check Yourself

- What methodology do I employ in my delivery of curriculum?

- Do I implement the explicit and implicit curriculum with fidelity as it was designed (the intent of the authors)?

- How successful is my instructional method for my students (using the 85% criteria)? What else do they need?

Fig. 5.1. Tier 1 Core Instruction

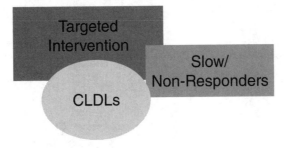

General Education
(Core Instruction)

Targeted Intervention

Slow/ Non-Responders

CLDLs

Use the guiding questions below (figure 5.2) and answer each as they apply to curriculum, instruction, and students' needs.

Fig. 5.2. Guiding Questions to Facilitate Inquiry and Decision Making Across the Three Domains

Question	Curriculum	Instruction	Student Needs
What is known about research validated practices?			
What is known about the needs of the students?			
Are the curricula and instructional strategies in place at present effective?			
Are the strategies we use matched to student needs?			
Is my core curriculum keeping 85% of my students at or above benchmark without accommodation or differentiation?			
Are we monitoring the extent to which the strategies and practices are effective?			
Am I implementing my core curriculum with complete fidelity?			
Do I end every school year with all of the students I began with, or do I have a high rate of student turnover (15% or more)?			

Scientifically Based Versus Scientifically Validated

In Chapter 3, *scientifically based* was defined as referring to curricula and practices that are founded on research. A good example would be getting the Report of the National Reading Panel and implementing a curriculum that references the research found in this report. *Scientifically validated* was defined as referring to the gold standard of practices, and more importantly, curricula. These are methods that have been repeatedly proven using a scientific approach to work. A scientifically validated curriculum will have been tested and verified by third parties (not the publishers) to confirm that it produces the outcomes it claims.

One of the first researchers to document and begin studying early low-reading achievement in students at risk was Juel (1988). Juel reported that approximately 88% of first-grade students whose performance scores were in the lower quartile in reading and comprehension remained at performance levels below the 50th percentile through the fourth grade. If your data reflects similar consistency, then you must consider the possibility that the Tier 1 instruction, the core curriculum, is not doing its job.

In a reading implementation showing strong success with CLDLs, the effectiveness of reading instruction for students at risk received in early school years is of "utmost importance" (Carlson and Francis 2002). Many others have since validated that explicit instruction using validated methodology and curriculum is an essential component for student success in an intervention setting. But program effectiveness was only "partially attributable to the content of the instructional program itself" (Carlson and Francis 2002). All three components (curriculum, instruction, and students' needs, as described above), determine the strength of an implementation.

Ponds and Oceans

One of the challenges faced in determining the strength of a proposed Tier 1 is whether it addresses local, state, or English language arts standards. Prior to the establishment of the Common

Core Standards, Standards were not standard among states. The definitions of *literacy* and *proficiency* varied among assessments, particularly if they were locally normed. Using locally-normed assessments is like comparing the sizes of fish in one pond, without considering fish in any other body of water. Local standards help to determine whether a program meets local criteria, but your screening and monitoring tools will tell you whether or not those standards cut it in the bigger scheme of things. Until full implementation of the Common Core Standards (anticipated in 2014), the best way to compare is to examine an annual review of education indicators for grades K–12 to see where your state falls as compared to other states.

If implementation of the core curriculum fails to keep 85% of students at or above benchmark on a nationally-normed screening device, it's time for a new core or extensive professional development in the existing program. If a new curriculum is the route you choose, look for a better scope and a more explicit sequence.

Practitioner's Perspective

During my first year of teaching at a chronically failing elementary school, I often found myself at my desk crying, seeking divine inspiration to carry me through another day. My sixth grade class was so far behind. The average reading level was hovering around mid-first grade. I could not understand why some of my colleagues who had been there for years did not seem up to the challenge of motivating the students to attempt to excel, or to even care about their grades. Where was intrinsic motivation? Teachers would say to me, "This is just where these kids are." These kids? It was as though they simply accepted that the pond we were in had its own ecosystem. The students who were squeaking by, almost at benchmark, were the big fish. My fear was what would happen to our big fish when they had to swim in the lake of a comprehensive high school? What would happen if and when they swam in the sea of a college, or the ocean of work life? Would they still be big fish?

What Works Is Not Whatever Works

The problem with the "whatever works" approach is that it is not consistent from one classroom to the next, nor is it replicable. Therefore, it cannot be validated. What truly works for CLDLs at risk will work in every classroom, and not just in the classrooms of highly skilled practitioners, but also in the classrooms of novice teachers who have received an elemental amount of professional development in the curriculum or methodology. Consider this: If you are sick, do you want the medication that sometimes works for some people, or the one that *always* works for *everyone?*

In the public education arena, the politics of education has often drowned out the evidence surrounding validated best practices. Teaching children to read is difficult, even though we know how to do it. In the past, we have heard teaching reading compared to rocket science, but perhaps practicing law presents a better comparison. It is multifaceted. It requires constant monitoring and review of past outcomes. No two clients are alike. Each brings a socio-cultural history that requires tailoring of practice, even if the essential elements of the process are the same. An attorney may start with a standard approach, but if things go downhill during trial, the attorney has to bring in more evidence, attack harder, and use stronger skills. No matter what, the desired outcome remains the same—victory. In the teacher's case it is defined as skilled reading.

A great deal of documentation exists on the academic plight of the at-risk student and the effectiveness of specific approaches to raising the academic achievement of the most needy children. Current approaches to teaching reading all profess to have the same general outcome—skilled reading. Yet, there are specific methods of instruction that reliably produce the desired gains and may be implemented with a quantifiable degree of fidelity to support achievement for students at-risk. Hopefully, your school has selected one with validation. If so, commit to using it with fidelity. If 85% of students are not meeting benchmarks with it, toss it and move further to the right on the pedagogical spectrum. If you are not in a position to throw it out, at least you can strengthen it. Consider the sequence of the critical components. Is it appropriately sequenced based on scientific research? If not, look to the research to help you align the sequence to what works. Does it rely on synthetic or analytic phonics? Again, rely on the science for tools to help you craft an appropriate delivery. Just remember, a failure to develop basic reading skills during the first few years of school has been shown to be "related to a number of academic, economic, and socio-emotional difficulties" (Carlson and Francis 2002).

Practitioner's Perspective

One of my favorite studies examined the Rodeo Institute for Teacher Excellence's implementation of a commercial curriculum and the professional development model that accompanied it. This effort was designed to raise the reading achievement of students placed at risk for reading failure in 20 elementary schools in Houston, Texas (Carlson and Francis 2002). Results indicated that the Rodeo Institute's unique combination of using a proven curriculum and providing ongoing professional development significantly increased reading achievement in students placed at risk when compared to a demographically matched control group over a four year period.

You may not have the opportunity to conduct a four-year, demographically matched scientific investigation of your reading curriculum and professional development model, but the good news is, you don't have to! Others have already done it and the published findings in numerous educational journals will provide you with the evidence and documentation you need to make a most informed decision.

Before delving into the research studies, always look to see who commissioned them. Independent, third-party efficacy studies take a more distanced stance when it comes to program evaluation.

Navigating Tier 1 Instruction

At the beginning of every school year, no doubt the first thing you do with all students is to assess them for difficulties. To do this requires a screening tool. The Tier 1 flow chart shown in figure 5.3 should help you navigate through the year with your Tier 1 students. All students get screened. For those students who are at or above proficient, begin instruction with the Tier 1 core curriculum. (Students who are not at proficient should follow the Tier 2 or Tier 3 flowchart in Chapter 6.)

After the initial screen, determine if 85% of students are performing at or above proficient levels. If yes, then the Tier 1 curriculum used during the previous year must have done its job. (Unless, of course, you teach kindergarten. In that case, the parents laid a firm foundation upon which you may begin building.) But, if fewer than 85% of students are at or above proficient, approach your administrator for an evaluation of the core curriculum.

Fig. 5.3. Instructional Flow Chart

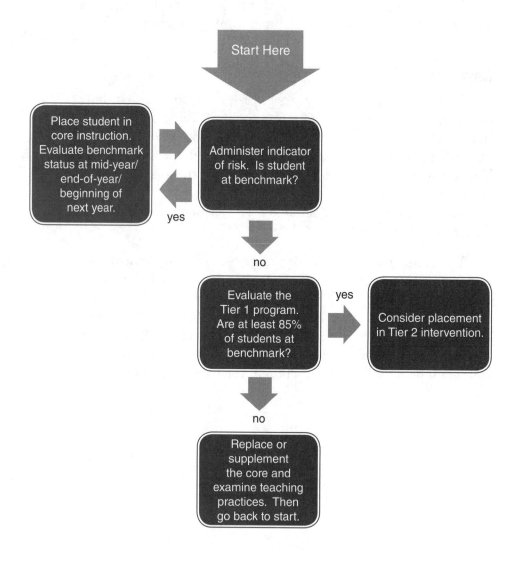

At mid-year, screen students again. Those who score at or above proficient may continue with core instruction. Those who have slipped should immediately be assessed for Tier 2 instruction. Again, determine if 85% of students are at or above proficient. If yes, fantastic! The Tier 1 curriculum is working. If fewer than 85% of students reached proficient, examine the curriculum and the instruction. Do not wait for failure. If fewer than 85% of students are at or above proficient, open up the discussion for evaluating the core curriculum, and look into professional development opportunities.

At the end of the year, perform one more screen. For those students who still score at or above proficient, recommend continuing with the core instruction the following year. Those that have slipped should begin the following year with an assessment for Tier 2 or Tier 3 instruction. Even better, assess for Tier 2 or Tier 3 placement at the end of the year so intensive instruction can begin at the beginning of the next year, without any delay. Again, refer to the 85% criteria.

Conclusion

Instruction involves three essential elements: curriculum, delivery, and student need. What is taught? How is it taught? How efficient, effective, and purposeful is the organization and planning? The model framework for implementation and some guiding questions for making decisions about curriculum and instruction (driven by the needs of students) is flexible and may be adapted for multiple content areas or whole school reform.

It serves no valid educational purpose to deliver content to which our children neither attend nor retain. Nor is it useful to spend months of each school year reviewing the content of the prior year. When that happens, the curriculum has been neither instructed nor learned, and that amounts to a wasted year for these students, who can least afford to waste any time whatsoever.

Are 85% of your children at or above proficient? Effective curriculum is only effective if the instructional delivery delivers on the promise of students mastering the concepts that were taught.

Reflect and Act

Evaluate your Tier 1 curriculum:

1. Examine the data for your students for the most recently completed year. (If your site does not use a multi-point screen, use a different assessment that is administered more than once during the year. For example, the chapter or unit tests for your Tier 1 curriculum.)

   a. What percentage of students met the benchmark at the beginning of the year?

   b. What percentage of students met the benchmark at the middle of the year?

   c. What percentage of students met the benchmark at the end of the year?

2. How did the levels of proficiency change over the course of the year? Do you have more students at proficient at the end of the year compared to the beginning (an upward trend that closes the gap)? Do you have more students falling into intervention categories (strategic, intensive, basic, below basic) over the course of the year (a downward trend indicating an increasing gap)?

3. If the data indicates a growing gap, a flat line, or fewer than 85% of students meeting benchmark, how can you begin the discussion about evaluating the core curriculum and instruction? To whom should your concerns be directed?

Chapter 6

Intensive Small Group Interventions

Recall the questions asked in Chapter 3. For the CLDLs at risk, they may not have the number of exposures to skilled reading at home as many other students do. In fact, we know that children of lower socioeconomic status come to school with a language deficit that hinders their acquisition of reading skills, placing them at risk (Hart and Risley 1995). Increased risks call for increased intensity of instruction.

For a student's mind to develop, it must be engaged. Learning is a process. The drill of certain information, or facts, may to some seem rote. However, neuroscience proves that massed and distributed practice at a high level of mastery, moves the processing of certain information and tasks to the frontal lobe. It is here that the hard work of learning occurs. Continued practice moves the information through the parietal lobe to the occipital lobe where automaticity happens. Dr. Sally Shaywitz (2003), in her work on students with dyslexia and the process of learning to read, proves this to be true. As we embark upon what Tier 2 and Tier 3 instruction necessitates for success, keep this in mind.

Practitioner's Perspective

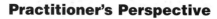

Throughout my life I have worn many hats, had a variety of adventures, and never hesitated to try something new. I began gymnastics and clarinet lessons in the fourth grade. In college I was a cheerleader and eventually a soldier in the U.S. Army. As I reflected on pedagogy and methodology, I noticed that all four of those significant ventures in my life had one methodology of teaching and learning in common: do it until you get it right, then do it some more. You see, practice does not make perfect—it makes permanent. It is only perfect practice that makes perfect. My clarinet teachers had no problem telling me I needed to work on a specific skill set to improve my playing (and hold on to that first chair position). My gymnastics instructors made me stretch every day. I distinctly remember wanting to be able to do a back handspring. I practiced and practiced until I could do it without hesitation. And then I did it another 30 or 40 times until it became ingrained in my muscle memory. I knew I had to keep doing it so I wouldn't lose it. We practiced our cheerleading routines every day, even the old ones, so we wouldn't mess up out on the field or court. And I can't even imagine how many times I broke down and reassembled my M-16 until I could do it blindfolded. The point is, spaced repetition with perfect practice to mastery is an acceptable approach to learning many skills. Why do we have a problem with the approach when it comes to teaching those most fundamental skills—skilled reading and mathematics?

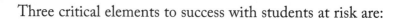

Three critical elements to success with students at risk are:

- implementing research-based practices in early reading instruction

- bringing sound research-based practices to scale

- overcoming obstacles for moving sustainable practices to scale (Foorman and Moats 2004).

This chapter deals with the first two of these elements. Foorman and Moats (2004) argued that explicitly developing critical reading skills through grade six was important for students across all socioeconomic levels. Consider, then, that cultural and linguistic diversity adds an additional factor of risk. If explicit instruction is good for all learners, it is even better for those with additional risk factors.

A skills-based curriculum, even though it may not be written to state or local standards, shows greater success with students at risk (Borman et al. 2002). Where students are at risk due to factors such as socioeconomic status and primary language, a scientifically based, research-validated curriculum is essential. Then, pair that with a CA-RTI model that emphasizes teaching with fidelity to the chosen core curriculum. Add progress monitoring using growth-oriented assessments, and the result should be higher levels of achievement on high-stakes, norm-referenced, and standards-based assessments over time. Achievement under a model similar to this CA-RTI model is illustrated by several well-founded studies (Borman et al. 2002; Carlson and Francis 2002; Gersten, Keating, and Becker 1988; Britton, Brooks-Gunn, and Griffin 2006; Kamps et al. 2007; and Slavin and Cheung 2003).

Using Small Groups

All Tier 2 and Tier 3 instruction requires small, homogeneous groups of students. Small-group instruction has been validated as being more efficient in terms of learning and acceleration of progress over one-on-one intervention (Elbaum et al. 1999). Even commercial Tier 2 and Tier 3 curricula suggest small-group instruction. Small groups typically number three to five. (Remember, if 85% of students are at or above proficient, you should only have, at most, two small groups for intervention; and that with a class of 30 students.)

Tier 2 and Tier 3: The Action Plan

Tier 2 and Tier 3 instruction is designed to close the gap and eliminate the risk of future failure for culturally and linguistically diverse learners. When it comes to CA-RTI, at these intensive tiers, seven components are critical for success. They are:

1. Use methods and strategies based on validated, scientific research.

2. Have a comprehensive design with components that are fully aligned.

3. Use measurable progress and benchmarks for students as an integral part of the decision-making progress.

4. Have a process for annual review (at minimum).

5. Identify your school and district resources for additional support.

6. Put a system of continuous high-quality professional development into place.

7. To ensure fidelity, employ experienced, high-quality external technical support.

The first four items can be done at the classroom level, although greater effectiveness comes with expansion across classrooms and grade levels throughout a school. Item five can be done at the classroom level, but it helps to have well-placed supporters that can increase the effectiveness of the implementation. Items six and seven really require a school- or district-level implementation and support. Vet your external support carefully. Not only do they need to know RTI, they need to understand the additional complexities of the cultural and linguistic diversity that you have in your classroom, at your school, or at your district.

The goal of Tier 2 and Tier 3 instruction is to close the gap within two years and no more. Your Tier 2 and Tier 3 curricula must include a scope and sequence of sufficient rigor to provide the necessary repetitions, massed and distributed practice of discrete and cumulative skills so that students are constantly cycling information in and out of short- and long-term memory.

The Tier 2 and Tier 3 curriculum must consider the overarching, big picture constructs that must be learned. However, it must deliver the information in incremental pieces of sequential development that will allow the student to not just learn about, but synthesize and evaluate, building new constructs from prior knowledge.

Tier 2 and Tier 3 are never about discovery learning. You, the teacher, are the model. You must provide immediate error detection and correction. You must ensure that extrinsic and program-designed intrinsic motivation occurs as a part of every lesson. Tier 2 and Tier 3 are intervention. All students must receive instruction at their academic level so that no student lags in learning; all groups are homogeneous.

No matter how explicit the curriculum is, it does not let the teacher off the hook for delivering with exceptional fidelity. It takes a skilled educator to guide students and to elicit the responses that will increase the pace and efficiency necessary to close the gap. Even scripted curriculum cannot be delivered well by a teacher with mediocre skills, and even the most explicit script does not drive the lesson. The teacher's knowledge of sequential skill development, and the recognition of true learning to mastery by students are the components that drive learning. In this sense, the delivery (instruction) and design (curriculum) share equal importance. The phenomenal deliverer, the phenomenal teacher, achieves the greatest gains.

Tier 2

Chapter 3 outlined the six components of the RTI round (figure 6.1). We will use the first four elements here to begin the examination of a Tier 2 curriculum.

Fig. 6.1. CA-RTI Flowchart

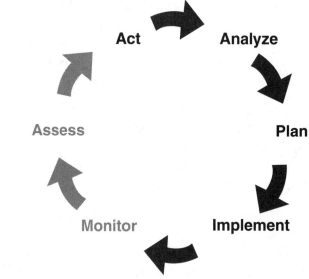

Step 1: Act

If you do not already have a Tier 2 curriculum in place, begin by investigating what is available within your school or district as an acceptable Tier 2. If you have been given *carte blanche*, contact educational publishers and inquire as to what Tier 2 curricula they have that meets the needs of your culturally and linguistically diverse population of struggling learners. Be explicit in expressing your needs. Get a good sampling of what's available. In searching for Tier 2 supplemental intervention, you are looking for more explicit instruction based on the identified weaknesses of your students. If they are having trouble with phonics, and your core instruction has an implied phonics approach, look for an analytical or synthetic phonics approach. Whatever the strand, you must look for materials that are evidenced or validated on student populations similar to your own that will fill the gap left by the core.

Step 2: Analyze

If you know that your Tier 1 instruction is not meeting the needs of a particular subset of your population, based on information from your screening measure, and perhaps a diagnostic or two, you may have an idea of the specific areas in which you need to focus. Keep in mind the seven ways to provide "*more*" during Tier 2 (from Chapter 3):

- more systematic
- more scaffolding
- more explicit
- more feedback
- more modeling
- more opportunities
- more examples

Tier 2 should not be a rehash of Tier 1, which did not work in the first place. It has to be better, stronger, and faster. No matter how cute, easy to implement, or teacher-friendly the instruction is, if it doesn't offer more to students, it is a waste of money and time. You may have the money, but students do not have the time.

Step 3: Plan

There is an old adage that says proper planning prevents poor performance. That is especially important here. You may find that you need to enlist the help of a colleague, particularly if this is a school-wide implementation. This is preferable, since sharing is one of the most important life skills that should be practiced for the benefit of our students. Break down this step into some subsets: who, what, and when. (We already know why, and RTI is the how.)

Who gets Tier 2 instruction? Who gets Tier 3? Tier 2 instruction is for students who have single skill deficits or are just slightly below grade level, i.e., students whose initial screening results place them at a strategic level of risk in one or two areas only. Tier 3 students have multiple deficits. Their screening results indicate that they need an intensive level of instruction in one or more areas. Tier 3 students may be two or more years below grade level.

Cross-grouping over grade levels provides an opportunity for more students to receive targeted instruction within more homogeneous groups. It is not practical or advisable to place first graders with fourth graders, however, it is fine to group first with without worrying about social issues. Middle school is a social issue in it's own right, but children at the middle and high school levels are in constant contact with one another across grades, so it is much less an issue. Keep in mind, though, that for the same reasons that kindergarteners have their own playground, they should be grouped only across kindergarten classrooms and not across grade levels.

One component of the planning will include when to teach intervention. When working across classrooms and grade levels, common teaching blocks are necessary in the elementary school. In the comprehensive middle and high schools, the master schedule rules all.

Consider the progress-monitoring component of the implementation. You will need a calendar that is agreed upon by all to monitor progress, analyze the data, and make decisions about changes to the groups, pacing, or curriculum based on that data. The Tier 2/Tier 3 flowchart shown later in figure 6.2 will help with the big picture plan. Still, there remains much to discuss with colleagues.

Teach intervention every day, five days a week, 180 instructional days per year. The more we teach, the faster the gap will close. Remember, Tier 2 is an additional 30 minutes per day in addition to the core instruction. Tier 3 is 90–120 minutes per day, supplanting the core instruction.

Step 4: Implement

Once the plan is in place, implement it with all deliberate speed and fidelity. Use the Tier 2 CA-RTI flowchart (figure 6.2) to help plan for monitoring and regrouping.

Fig. 6.2. Tier 2 and Tier 3 CA-RTI Flow Chart

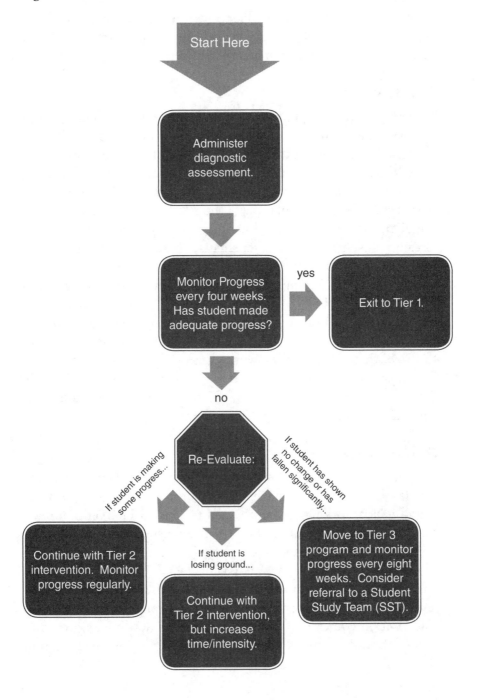

Start Here

Administer diagnostic assessment.

Monitor Progress every four weeks. Has student made adequate progress?

yes

Exit to Tier 1.

no

Re-Evaluate:

If student is making some progress...

If student has shown no change or has fallen significantly...

Continue with Tier 2 intervention. Monitor progress regularly.

If student is losing ground...

Continue with Tier 2 intervention, but increase time/intensity.

Move to Tier 3 program and monitor progress every eight weeks. Consider referral to a Student Study Team (SST).

Tier 3

Stepping it up a notch to Tier 3 instruction, continue to rely on the first four steps of the RTI round that we used for Tier 2. At this stage, though, everything is maximized.

Step 1: Act

If you don't already have a Tier 3 curriculum in place, begin by investigating what is available within your school or district. Talk to the special education team. They often have a wealth of knowledge that goes untapped by the general education teachers, and they are usually quite willing to help. Make certain any purchased Tier 3 curricula meets the needs of your culturally and linguistically diverse population of struggling learners. If you have already chosen your Tier 2 curricula, share that information as well. Again, be very explicit in expressing your needs. Sometimes a little creativity is required. Research grants to fund curriculum materials. Consider collaborating with a local university that does educational research. They might bring you materials and researchers who will help with delivery and validation procedures to prove that the measures worked. Also, publishers often look for classrooms to field test materials and provide feedback. Be flexible and obtain permission from administrators and your leadership team. (Consider giving them a copy of this book.)

Step 2: Analyze

Some of your Tier 2 students may fall into Tier 3 over the course of the year. Again, this is an opportunity to analyze what is and is not working for your students. Tier 3 intervention must have a higher degree of structure and intensity than Tier 2. Tier 3 students will be homogeneous, but the multiple skill deficits are typically all over the map. View your Tier 3 groups on a broader spectrum, in terms of how many years they are below grade level. Provide Tier 3 students with the strongest, most focused intervention you can get your hands on in order to bring them to grade level. Remember, Tier 3 is about offering the maximum in terms of:

- time
- opportunities for practice and review
- correction and feedback
- engaged time on-task

- repetition and review
- breakdown of tasks into discrete, small steps
- visibility of learning
- prompting and cueing

Step 3: Plan

Much of the Tier 2 plan will flow into Tier 3. Sharing resources is even more important in Tier 3. Since you can still cross groups over grade levels, instructional time becomes the greater issue here, because Tier 3 should replace the Tier 1 instruction.

Practitioner's Perspective

There is a lot of push-back on the idea of supplanting versus supplementing curriculum at Tier 3; I always ask, what works? It's always about a philosophy or policy. How much would we learn with "exposure to grade level content"? (Recall the quantum physics example from Chapter 3.) Tier 3 students may have suffered long-term failure being "exposed" to a curriculum to which they have no real access. Who is served by this type of instruction? Replace or supplant. Do not supplement!

Only by replacing the Tier 1 core can we ensure that students make the significant gains necessary when they are several years below grade level. In a presentation, Tim Shanahan pronounced, "Amount of teaching is the most important, alterable determinant of learning" (Shanahan 2005, slide 4). I wrote that on a sticky note and stuck it above my desk. Students in Tier 3 need as much instructional time at their instructional level as possible. If we can get out of our philosophical and procedural comfort zones for a few years, we could do amazing things for students most at risk.

Step 4: Implement

Tier 3 requires the strongest possible curriculum and instruction in considering scope and sequence. For Tier 3, use these guidelines for strength:

- Skills should be developed through massed and distributed practices which later combine to form higher-order thinking skills.

- Learned skills should be continuously reviewed and practiced to mastery as new skills are integrated.

- Lessons should be completely predictable; do not throw the students any curve balls.

- Any commercial curriculum should have field test validation for students that match your demographic. This is particularly true when working with CLDLs whose background knowledge and linguistics may challenge learning in programs that are not designed for, or tested in, like demographics.

Instruction must be organized for the benefit of the learner. Although this is somewhat covered through the homogeneous grouping, it does not end there. Tier 3 instruction, maximized instruction, means actively teaching, bell-to-bell, for 90–120 minutes each day. This is not "worksheet and independent reading" time. This is "fully engaged, all students on task, teacher on his or her feet, students in their seats" time. Instructional pacing is critical. The better the pace, the more content is covered. Assessment of learning occurs throughout the course of each lesson. If you notice that your learners are struggling, do not move on. Fix the problem immediately. In Tier 3 intervention the teacher must:

- know each student as an individual

- creatively motivate students through instructional delivery

- add appropriate motivation based on the needs of individuals and the group

- carefully monitor skill development to adjust lesson pace, quantity of practice, and other needs-based elements

Tier 3 instruction should provide an integrated system of effective instructional practices, sophisticated curriculum design, and cautious monitoring of student progress. The flow chart for Tier 3 (figure 6.3) along with the progress-monitoring calendar in Chapter 4 (pages 73 and 74) should provide some support. If at all possible, choose a program with ongoing in-program assessments to provide feedback on the effectiveness of teaching and adequacy of student skill development for possible acceleration of instruction and regrouping of students.

Two Steps Forward, Then Start Over

For both Tier 2 and Tier 3, Step 5 is to monitor, and Step 6 is to reassess; after which, return to Step 1. Establish and follow a monitoring and assessment calendar. In addition, monitor and assess your own fidelity to the instruction. A number of schools and districts have self-monitoring periodic review forms that can be used for this purpose. Self-review is instrumental in determining whether the Tier 1 instruction is really working. With those questions asked and answered, with a full year of RTI under your belt, you then return to the planning stage.

Check Yourself

- Are students making progress towards closing the achievement gap?

- Am I legitimately reducing the number of students needing Tier 2 and Tier 3 interventions?

- Am I teaching with fidelity to the curriculum?

- When students advance to Tier 1 from Tier 2, do they stay there or regress?

Fig. 6.3. Tier 3 CA-RTI Flowchart

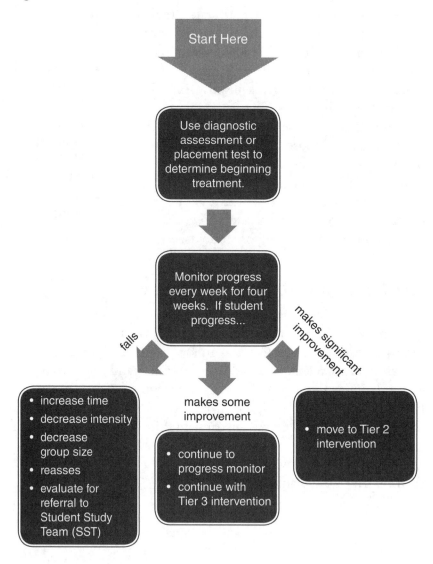

Technology

You may be wondering, "What about computer-based instructional components?" Technology certainly has its place in teaching and learning. It can play a prominent role in RTI, but it cannot replace a teacher when it comes to delivery of instruction. Technology can be used for additional practice and review. It can be used for recording fluency assessments. Amazing technology components exist for assessment and screening. However, approach the purchase and implementation of teaching software with great caution. A curriculum software that has been validated to produce measured gains for culturally and linguistically diverse children is not readily available. The use of software for additional assistance with reading fluency could show great promise within a CA-RTI model, provided it supplements, not supplants, Tier 2 and Tier 3 instruction. The ultimate outcome is increased achievement. "More transparent access to data...leads to the development and exchange of meaningful information" (Golden 2005). If you desire instructional technology, it should address teaching and learning. Allow all academic stakeholders at the school and district level the ability to quickly determine the effectiveness of instruction based on readily available data, and be sure it is updated frequently.

Technology should provide specific, targeted instruction with remediation activities based on the results of assessments, it can reduce the burden of assessment and monitoring, make your assessments and monitors more precise, and return your results faster. Some technology has exciting and visual game formats that encourage children to engage in skills-supported play, making additional practice more a reward than a challenge. But in the end, can you implement your CA-RTI without technology? Absolutely.

Conclusion

A great deal of work must be done when beginning or evaluating an implementation, but this is the bulk of what you need to know about RTI basics. This chapter offered tools for determining which students need something more and how much more they need. Use the calendar template to begin to make concrete plans to put a solid school or district-wide program into place. Language and cultural diversity issues create an extra layer of challenge for CLDL students in an RTI implementation. Next, we will address how to pair intervention and language acquisition.

Reflect and Act

Before reviewing these questions, consider whether you are just beginning to put a plan into place or are evaluating a plan in the second or later year.

1. What curriculum do you currently have in place?

2. Compare your Tier 2 choices to the core. Compare the Tier 3 choices to the Tier 2 and Tier 1 (core) curricula. How well do they correlate? If the correlation is not strong, outline a comprehensive plan to act.

3. Assess your instruction. Are students getting closer to closing the achievement gap?

4. Is there a reduction in the number of students needing Tier 2 and Tier 3 interventions?

5. Is there fidelity to the curriculum?

6. When students move from Tier 2 to Tier 1, do they stay there or regress?

Chapter 7

Teaching English as an Explicit Language

> *"There is no equality of treatment merely by providing students with the same facilities, textbooks, teachers, and curriculum; for students who do not understand English are effectively foreclosed from any meaningful education."*

> —*Justice Brennan, Lau v. Nichols*
> *(414 U.S. 563)*

CLDLs are no longer the invisible children. Change requires networks of relationships to develop, common causes to be sought out, and a vision to develop (Wheatley and Frieze 2007). Large scale change comes about as connections, interactions, and interdependencies develop and strengthen. The result will be a powerful cultural shift that influences our behaviors as educators and defines the practices acceptable for culturally and linguistically diverse learners. Like religion and politics, some debates are just plain dangerous in polite and diverse company. When it comes to the future of America's CLDLs we should stop debating and take positive action based on the science. CA-RTI must become the ideology of American education if we are to fulfill the vision of achievement for all children.

Once you have determined that the structure of CA-RTI is in place at your school, it is time to harmoniously combine instructing for cultural appropriateness, increasing students' basic interpersonal communication skills (BICS), and increasing cognitive academic language proficiency (CALP). CA-RTI must provide an accord between the cultural and the cognitive aspects of instruction, eliminating the BICS-CALP gap.

Practitioner's Perspective

Over the years that I have been in the K–12 educational arena, I have witnessed a battle between two frequently competitive communities. One community deals with the acquisition of language for English language learners. The other community focuses on intervention and the achievement gap that grows when students do not get appropriate cognitive growth. Like the Hatfields and the McCoys, it is a feud that has waged for years. One of my goals has been to declare a truce, marry the two, and increase the academic achievement of all CLDLs in the process.

History of the Divide

To date, despite repeated attempts from the Progressive Era in education through the current Age of Accountability, the dilemma over how best to provide educational services to culturally and linguistically diverse learners persists. Immigration has been pervasive throughout American history. Each wave of immigration brings to the American educational system a recurrence of issues regarding language of instruction, methodology, and axiology. Historical, social, and philosophical foundations and philosophies exist across a broad spectrum approaching this recurrent and contemporary issue.

One may trace educational reform from the Great Wave to the present and find that little has changed or improved regarding the instructional practices and achievement of culturally and linguistically diverse learners. What one does not learn from history, one is doomed to repeat. Consider the attempts of the last 25 years. The push towards tough standards, academic excellence, and teaching all students to use higher cognitive skills dominated the 1980s. During the tenure of President Ronald Reagan, the National Commission on Educational Excellence published the findings of their study—*A Nation At Risk* (U. S. Department of Education 2003)—outlining the factors that had led to the demise of public education and what must be rectified. Yet, as one examines the record of achievement for CLDLs, one sees slow to no growth.

Since the early days of public education, American schools have consistently served one purpose: to acculturate culturally and linguistically diverse children into the middle-class Anglo-Protestant core values and norms (Pai, Adler, and Shadow 2005; Tozer, Violas, and Senese 2002). Gutek (1997) wrote, "While it served the aims of nation building, public schooling as a means of social control often disregarded linguistic, ethnic, and cultural pluralism." Schools have always been charged with being the social levelers.

Schools continually face the pedagogical and political issues surrounding instruction of culturally and linguistically diverse learners' acquisition of English language through a variety of instructional models. How do we best create English speakers? Is it through bilingual instruction? English immersion? English language development? And do these instructional methods preserve the heritage language? Should they? These issues have been historically debated, but never fully resolved (Pai, Adler, and Shadow 2005; Tozer, Violas, and Senese 2002). The White Anglo-Saxon Protestant ideology of American democracy and capitalism counter the culturally pluralistic ideal of preservation of heritage languages in American education. The debate has worked to foster the establishment and growth of the Catholic and Jewish school systems, private schools, magnet schools, charter schools, and others who value the preservation of heritage language and development of bilingual, biliterate, bicultural children.

Like the Great Wave of Immigration, the current level of immigration into America's educational system brings an increase in attendance at public schools from non-traditionally served populations (Tozer, Violas, and Senese 2002). The current strain of immigrant and culturally and linguistically diverse learners is seen by the political status quo just as the great waves of immigrants were viewed before them: as unwelcome, and/or of a lesser quality of persons than preferred (Pai, Adler, and Shadiow 2005; Tozer, Violas, and Senese 2002). *Plyler v. Doe,* 457 U.S. 202 (1982) guaranteed a free public education to illegally resident children in the United States; however, the axiological and political implications of such an education are far-reaching and multifaceted. In the current Age of Accountability under federal mandates, court orders, and No Child Left Behind, the public outcries over teaching, learning, student readiness, and ability that were raised during the Great Wave are currently echoed in response to the strain placed on public education as of 2011.

Why the History Matters

The No Child Left Behind Act, unprecedented in its scope, has brought accountability into American education as no other act of government before. Schools can no longer hide the shortcomings of immigrant children in overall achievement data. The microscope has been focused, and change may no longer receive mere lip service. We must examine the history of immigrant education, social implications of immigrant education, and the philosophical foundations that influence the various ideological approaches to curriculum and instruction of immigrant children in America today if we are to improve our practice for tomorrow.

Examine how philosophy has influenced education throughout America's history. There is a link between the ideologies and culture of those who control the educational system—the *status quo*—and the enculturation of culturally and linguistically diverse learners. Then, examine the reforms and rebukes that have been enacted as educational policy, designed to acculturate CLDLs when enculturation did not occur rapidly enough. Take this prime example: We delineate proficiency testing and disaggregation of data by demographic. Without passing judgment, I would like to suggest we at least examine the rationale for this—what's behind the curtain?

In the Best Interest of All Stakeholders

Some argue that those in control of the schools hold jurisdiction over two critical components of education. The first is access to information: *who* gets taught. The second is the criterion that determines what type of knowledge is valid, valued, and legitimate: *what* gets taught (DeMarrais and LeCompte 1999). America is seen as a land of opportunity "where all can succeed if they try" (Wheatley and Frieze 2007). Some students, because of cultural and linguistic diversity, are more of a challenge to teach, especially if they are being taught without offering them true access to the necessary information in a way that is culturally relevant for them. This is one problem with "exposure to grade-level curriculum" when children are not even at grade level. Access and content criterion are mismatched to the needs of the students. Every child merits an education. Providing that education is much more difficult for those teachers tasked with the instruction of some students who have more hurdles to clear than others.

The relationship between school and society requires analysis of myriad interactions: between students, teachers, administrators, and the various peer groups in the school system (Pai, Adler, and Shadiow 2005). Closing the achievement gap improves America. Sameness of facilities, textbooks, teachers, and curriculum, while helpful, is insufficient to fully close this gap. Children at risk require more and better—more qualified teachers, better curriculum, and implementation of the most scientifically based, research-validated pedagogies and methods, implemented with absolute fidelity. Schools must focus their attention on the most fragile students if access is for all, and content is to be delivered with mastery for all learners.

How Long Does it Take to Learn English?

The answer to this question is unclear. Language acquisition experts have provided ranges from a minimum of four to a maximum of nine years (Cummins 1984; Thomas and Collier 2001). However, many questions arise. Are we talking about learning English to a basic level of operational proficiency? Are we talking about learning English at a level commensurate with high-achieving students at each age and grade? And don't some monolingual students have low-language proficiency even though their only language is English? The answer is yes to all of the above. If we consider basic language development of our own children, it took four to six years before they spoke English at a level that other adults could readily understand. Language acquisition has a correlated relationship to language exposure.

Language Acquisition

It is critical to clarify the two types of language acquisition applied in education: BICS and CALP. Cummins (1979) first coined these acronyms to refer to the two different aspects of language acquisition faced by immigrant children. BICS are basic interpersonal communication skills. This is language used in social discourse. You may think of students who come to your classroom with little or no command of English, and yet they begin to converse with their peers very rapidly. They are acquiring BICS which is often referred to as "playground English" or "survival English". BICS is basic language ability that is highly contextualized and often accompanied by gestures. BICS require a low cognitive demand, are context embedded, and much more easily and quickly acquired than CALP, or Cognitive Academic Language Proficiency. CALP requires, as the name indicates, a higher cognitive demand. Academic language is the language of classroom lecture and instruction.

Fig. 7.1. Language Proficiency Matrix

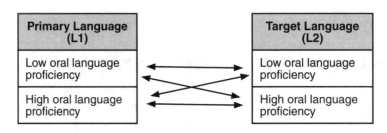

Practitioner's Perspective

One year, a student came into my class midway through the fall semester. Nasreen had just come to the United States from Pakistan, spoke almost no English, and had very little formal schooling. Her primary language was Urdu. To say I had no familiarity with the language would be a gross understatement. Nor could I find anyone in a school district of more than 35,000 students to provide primary language assistance. The only viable academic option was to teach English, and teach it as quickly as possible. Nasreen was a sponge. She soaked up every bit of language and content instruction provided. In spite of no exposure to English at home, by the end of her sixth grade year, she had BICS competency and grade four CALP. Now, here's the funny thing. My grade level employed an extremely punitive model of RTI. At that time, there was no such thing as RTI. Still, all of our students received targeted instruction in reading based on their proficiency levels. Nasreen began in a group that performed at about a first grade level. My question at the time was, "Why was she able to gain both BICS and CALP in English at the same rate as her English-only peers?" Was it due to her motivation? Aptitude? Expectations? How about instruction? With no method to provide primary language support, scientifically validated reading instruction that included explicit instruction in the language of English was the only tool in the toolbox. The tool worked. Nasreen was not the only student who made similar gains in BICS and CALP in that school, nor was Urdu the sole primary language for which the approach was used. This same approach of explicit, systematic instruction of reading in English has been validated in languages as diverse as Somali, Sudanese, Vietnamese, and Spanish (Kamps et al. 2007). I use Nasreen as an example because so frequently educators are allowed to fall back on the excuse that a lack of primary language support, time, or an ELD-specific curriculum prevents students from making adequate yearly progress. I say, hogwash to that!

Many other questions will pop into your head as you begin to ponder and reflect upon the initial baselines and progress made in terms of language acquisition of your own students. Consider the matrix in figure 7.1. It is very simplistic, but students can be low-low, low-high, high-low, or high-high. The combination of proficiencies in Primary Language (L1) and Target Language (L2) will affect not only a student's rate of L2 acquisition, both BICS and CALP, but also his or her rate of reading proficiency.

What Is Involved in a Language Proficiency Assessment?

What are the tools frequently used to determine language proficiency? First, it involves a great deal of data analysis in order to set goals and establish instructional groupings for intensive intervention. A frequently encountered frustration is the lack of correlation between assessments used by the district to determine language development levels for English language learners (ELLs). Ideally, an English language development assessment should determine a student's need for sheltered instruction. In many instances, students who consistently score at benchmark on screening and progress monitoring devices and speak English beautifully still classify as non-English speaking. Why? Curriculum-based measurements must reflect the development of linguistic processes. Studies on assessment reliability and validity by Abedi (2004) indicate that academic achievement tests normed for native, standard English speakers have a lower reliability and validity for ELLs. Many measures of language proficiency do not have enough evidence of trustworthiness to validate their use (Kame'enui et al. 2006). Time and resources may be wasted in assessing students with inappropriate tools, without ever providing the information necessary to change outcomes in language development and overall reading skills.

In one urban district, students whose bilingual verbal ability and English language proficiency assessments scores indicated an English language development (ELD) level of one or two (on a five-point scale) received an alternate curriculum thought to be a better fit for English language learners. That curriculum moved much more slowly and provided much less rigor than the standard core (Pray 2005). (See Chapter 5 for a discussion of core curriculum rigor.)

A three-year trend data indicated a continually increasing academic gap for English language learners placed in that alternate core compared to demographically similar peers in the rigorous core curriculum. Two elements were at work here. One, less rigor resulted in fewer gains. The choice of a less rigorous curriculum for students at a greater risk resulted in growing a gap rather than closing one. Secondly, in this instance, the assessment measured cognition rather than language proficiency (Pray 2005). The resulting student placement, based on that assessment, provided less opportunity for building a strong academic foundation: dysteachia at its finest.

The assumption that "different is better" for linguistically diverse students is often inaccurate. Schools ought to define and provide a solid, scientific rationale for using a different curriculum. Earlier chapters addressed several recommendations by August and Shanahan (2006) for providing instruction to CLDLs and ELLs. Two more recommendations, providing extensive and varied vocabulary instruction and developing academic English, appear below. These are accomplished through explicit teaching, interactive instruction, and instruction geared towards lower performers. Keep those in mind as we move into the discussion of English learning, phonemic awareness and decoding, and vocabulary development.

English Learning

It seems obvious that teachers should provide explicit instruction in English in order to improve the English learning of CLDLs. But make no assumptions that this is taking place. Some cognates exist for mapping (primarily the Romance languages) to English; however, that assumes learners have high oral-language proficiency in L1. What if they do not? Not only must you provide the content of instruction, you must teach English. Think back to the language classes you had in high school. Learning the language was facilitated by placing new words on a pre-existing schema. If children are in that upper left quadrant of low oral language proficiency in L1, they may lack the schema for vocabulary, content, and even the structure of language. This is true not only of English language learners, but culturally diverse English-only students, as well.

Practitioner's Perspective

I once observed a second-grade classroom while the teacher frontloaded vocabulary for a story. I became increasingly frustrated at the agonizing six-minute schema activation. The students did not have story-specific schema to activate. The teacher failed to recognize the absence. Finally, a little girl quietly said, "Why don't you show us a picture?"

Facilitate instruction for low oral-language proficiency students through the use of visuals or manipulatives to teach content. A picture is worth a thousand words. For example, a group of high school students might have a very specific visual image of a gold digger, based on popular culture but it might be very different from the one in their textbook on the California Gold Rush. Most likely, it would be an image that they have seen in a hip-hop music video. Our students are growing up in a very visual and kinesthetic world. While we need to develop stronger verbal and auditory processing skills, the economics of instructional time allows for valid shortcuts. Show them the picture. Give them concrete objects to see, touch, smell, and examine.

Encourage students to give elaborate responses. Encourage them to make connections between the concepts taught and other aspects of their worlds. Recall Krashen's (1982) hypothesis of comprehended input. Teachers can assess students' language proficiency on-the-fly if students stretch to elaborate as much as possible when responding. The hypothesis contends that input is made comprehensible through context that supports its meaning.

If students cannot elaborate, there is a possibility that the instruction is not understood. Naturally, degrees of elaboration vary based on language proficiency, but teach students as much as they can absorb, plus a little bit more. Then, demand as much as possible back from them—all they can give, plus a little bit more.

Colleagues and friends joke that I would be unable to talk with my hands tied behind my back or my face covered. Not that I want to, but the point is, through gestures and facial expressions, teachers convey more information during instruction. Not all of these movements exist in every culture. In employing this strategy, teachers not only teach vocabulary and content, but also aspects of "mainstream American" culture.

Directly Teaching Key Vocabulary

Vocabulary development begins with birth and does not stop. Vocabulary instruction should not be an isolated element of the school day. It must occur across content areas and throughout each lesson. There are four specific caveats for vocabulary instruction with CLDLs in a CA-RTI model:

1. Teach difficult vocabulary prior to, and during, every lesson.

2. Provide systematic instruction for vocabulary development.

3. Structure multiple opportunities for students to use the lesson vocabulary throughout the day.

4. Engage students in meaningful interaction about the concepts.

First, recognize that all vocabulary words are not created equal, nor should they be taught equally. Beck, McKeown, and Kucan's (2002) work on tiered vocabulary instruction should play an integral role in your vocabulary instruction and focus for CLDLs. Beck et al., provided us with a system of word classification that has three tiers. Tier One words are basic words. They are high in utility and generally transfer from one language or culture to another. Tier Two words are words learners must understand in order to comprehend specific pieces of literature, particularly in the English language arts. While Tier Two words may be high-frequency words for mature speakers, their connection to specific times, places, or cultures in literature requires instruction for CLDLs. Tier Three words are the specialty words of the content areas. Each of the three tiers may require explicit instruction for CLDLs, and the following approach is appropriate, no matter the tier. Teaching difficult vocabulary and concepts prior to a lesson is known as *front-loading*. If your lesson calls for you to activate schema that your students do not have, you must teach it. Here are some suggestions for activating schema:

- Use strategies such as total physical response to teach verbs and many adverbs.

- Use photo libraries and picture dictionaries to provide graphic images so that students may make quick connections to things in their environments, or build initial schema for objects for which they have no connections.

- Use line drawings or multiple photographic images for more generalized concepts. For example, the noun *truck* could conjure up the image of a light pick-up or an 18-wheeler. Showing students several types of trucks allows them to generalize the concept.

- Use the environment whenever possible. Looking out the classroom window, how many trucks can students see on the street?

Make certain students have a preliminary knowledge of the vocabulary required to comprehend the coming instruction.

Practitioner's Perspective

During my first year of teaching a unit on Czarist Russia, I introduced the word dumas in print. Unfortunately, I did not introduce it correctly within a context, and my Cambodian boys just rolled with laughter. At first I thought that perhaps my poor spellers had mistaken it for two connected English words I heard them utter quite frequently. Then I realized my Cambodian girls appeared horrified, and my English-only poor spellers had not made the same connection. Later, one of my Cambodian girls told me that it was a very bad word in their language. Front-loading those types of terms within a context is essential. The next year I started with a connection to the United States Congress and a picture. That worked much better.

During the lesson, vocabulary instruction continues. Every time a front-loaded word or concept appears, check for comprehension. This does not mean asking students if they remember what a truck is. Students may nod, yes, but may not be telling the truth. Here is an example of how to front-load the vocabulary word *truck* (Engelmann and Osborn 2008): (Do not be fooled by the simplicity of this example. Think of the basic concept.)

> **Teacher** *(introduce the word* **truck***)*: Everybody, our first vocabulary word is *truck*. What is the word?
>
> **Students** *(in unison)*: Truck.
>
> **Teacher:** *(shows images of trucks and vehicles that are not trucks.)*: A truck is a vehicle that can be used to carry or pull large objects.
>
> **Students** *(as a group)*: A truck is a vehicle that can be used to carry or pull large objects. *(Teacher makes sure they can say it fluently.)*

During the lesson, when the word truck appears, check whether students remember the definition by asking the whole class, "Tell me the sentence we learned about a truck." To which the class should be able to respond in unison, "A truck is a vehicle that can be used to carry or pull large objects."

The second stipulation of vocabulary development calls for systematic instruction. As simple as the truck example may be for us as adults, students developing language need consistency. This example shows a basic format for introducing many words and concepts. Building on this example, we not only want students to know what a concept is, but also what it is not. You must provide nonexamples along with your examples. Show a car, a boat, a horse, a bicycle, and a mop. Initially, state that each of these items is not a truck. Later, you can stop telling and start asking, "Is this a truck?" while showing pictures of the nonexamples.

To build on this systematic method, structure opportunities for students to speak English. In our truck example, by asking for responses in unison, you will know which students do, and do not, know the definition. If you call only on students who raise their hands, you only have information about one or two students.

Three strategies for encouraging students to speak the vocabulary include ask-backs, flip-flops, and stretchers. An ask-back means asking students to say the part of the sentence that defines the concept. In the truck example, the conversation would look something like this:

Teacher: What is a truck?

Students: A vehicle that can be used to carry or pull large objects.

Flip-flops turn the sentence around and ask the students to do a bit more thinking about the language. An example of a flip-flop would be:

Teacher: What is a vehicle that can be used to carry or pull large objects?

Students: A truck.

Teacher: What can a truck do?

Students: A truck can carry or pull large objects.

Stretchers require students to build on prior knowledge and shape schema with the new concept. An example of a stretcher would be:

Teacher: Can a truck pull a car?

Students: Yes.

Teacher: Can a truck carry a refrigerator?

Students: Yes.

Teacher: When I call on you, tell me one more thing a truck can carry or pull. *(Calls on three to five students.)*

Teacher: When I call on you, tell me another vehicle that is like a truck and why they are alike. *(Calls on three to five students.)*

This method of vocabulary development allows the student to bring in knowledge about his or her own environment. Information that is relevant to the child is more culturally appropriate than our limited knowledge of concepts from our world and culture. This method relies on more interaction and language use on the part of the child. Teachers may provide the initial examples of language, but students must then build actively, engaging in the lesson, rather than passively receiving instruction. This method engages students in meaningful interactions.

- -

Theory to Practice

Identify three tiers of vocabulary in the text you use. Choose a selection of text from any material you currently use in your classroom. This can be a literature selection or a content-area selection. Skim the selection looking for words you may need to teach your students. Write those words in the matrix (figure 7.2) below.

Fig. 7.2. Identify Vocabulary

Tier 1 Words (Basic/High Utility)	Tier 2 Words (Text Selection Specific)	Tier 3 Words (Content Specific)

- -

Following the truck example above, create your own student-friendly definition for one or two of the Tier 2 and Tier 3 words. What sentences would you use to introduce them? What images, realia, or actions would you use to give students a visual, tactile, or kinesthetic experience? What nonexamples would you need for clarification? The truck example is simplistic, but the method will work on most vocabulary. With practice, it is an effective technique.

Once you have those student-friendly definitions, work out

some ask-backs and flip-flops, and integrate using key vocabulary throughout the day. Your students will be well prepared for The Vocabulary Game.

The Vocabulary Game

Directions: Work from a list of words you provide, or use a current text selection. Have students hold their fingers in the air. Randomly recite a definition for one of the words. Ask students to touch the word in the book, then to say the word.

Here is an example of how The Vocabulary Game works using the word *gravity*.

> **Teacher:** Time for The Vocabulary Game. Working from your science text, put your fingers in the air. Here is the definition: "the natural force of attraction between any two massive bodies." Listen again: "the natural force of attraction between any two massive bodies." Keep those fingers in the air until I count to three. One...two...three! Everybody, what's the word?

> **Students:** Gravity.

> **Teacher:** What is *gravity?*

> **Students:** The natural force of attraction between any two massive bodies.

> **Teacher:** Yes. Gravity is the natural force of attraction between any two massive bodies.

This approach may be inserted during reading instruction as a way to check word knowledge. It may be used to review the prior day's instruction before beginning the next lesson. The key is to make sure that all students respond, so that you know who does and who does not know the definition. As usual, remember the rule: 85% of students at benchmark.

BICS and CALP

The current body of research supports the instruction of CLDLs with scientifically-based reading researched programs, even prior to their developing language proficiency in English. The implemented curriculum must allow for the linguistic processes of developing language and the teaching of core content to CLDLs. A number of similarities exist in instruction for English language learners, CLDLs, and English proficient learners. Slavin and Cheung (2003) concluded that strong similarities exist between effective beginning reading programs for English language learners and those for English proficient children. They concluded that English language learners benefit from reading instruction that utilizes explicit, systematic phonics. Starting there, we can expand upon the population to include all CLDLs.

Phonemic Awareness Instruction for all CLDLs

Phonemic awareness indicates basic early literacy. Students must understand that sentences comprise complete thoughts. Sentences are made up of words. Words are made of letters. The ability to hear the sounds in orally presented words and to segment and blend those sounds orally are indicators of basic early literacy. Developing high fluency in phonemic awareness promotes fluency in reading *consonant-vowel-consonant (cvc), consonant-vowel-consonant + e (cvce), and consonant-vowel-vowel-consonant (cvvc)* words in kindergarten decodable reading. When the brain fluently processes sounds in the proper order, it builds automaticity. Automaticity reduces the risk of developing reading related disorders such as dyslexia and disfluency, which break and interrupt the flow of reading. Simply put, to learn to read fluently, students have to be able to fluently receive and express, and hear and speak, sounds, words, and sentences. Phonemic awareness instruction can be effective even when English language learners are not fluent English proficient (Argüelles 2005).

There are theories that suggest withholding English reading instruction until children are orally proficient in English (L2). Unfortunately, when as many as 20 different languages are spoken at a school site, there is no way to offer primary language reading instruction to all students. In fact, current research refutes that philosophy. Argüelles (2005) and others (Geva and Wang 2001; Linan-Thompson et al. 2003) have clearly established that not only does phonemic awareness transfer across phonetic languages, but English language learners can learn phonemic awareness and decoding skills when provided with research-based reading instruction. Therefore, teachers do not need to wait for English proficiency to develop prior to beginning reading instruction (Linan-Thompson et al. 2003).

Francis (2005) suggested that language and literacy could be built concurrently. Like Slavin and Cheung (2003), Gersten and Geva (2003), Argüelles (2005), and others all suggested that teachers adjust instruction for language ability. Academic oral language, CALP, must be stimulated and stretched during instruction. Griffin (1991) describes how Bandura believed that vicarious learning made strong gains once the student developed conscious awareness, or *metacognition*, of techniques used to teach and learn. Phonemic awareness fosters such metacognition.

The BICS-CALP Gap

Four domains of BICS and CALP are sociocultural, academic, cognitive, and linguistic. These four domains are interdependent (see figure 7.3).

A student's overall growth and future success depend on developing all of these components simultaneously (Collier 1995). Does that development stem from nature or nurture? It has often

Fig. 7.3. Domains of BICS and CALP

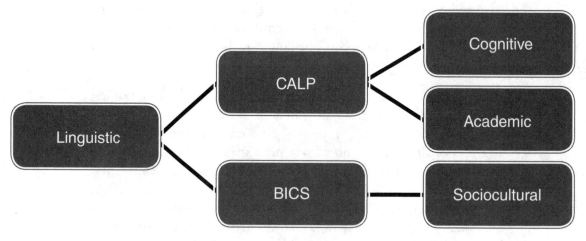

been mistakenly assumed that children learn languages more easily and quickly than adults. However, research has shown that adolescents and adults perform better than young children (August and Shanahan 2006, McLaughlin 1992, Newport 1990). Even when the method of teaching appears to favor learning in children, they do not perform as well as older language learners. Why? Return to the four quadrants in figure 7.1. Does the learner have high- or low-language proficiency in L1? Does the learner have high- or low-language proficiency in L2? If the child has lower L1 CALP, they may not develop L2 CALP as quickly, because they do not have the schema upon which to hang new words.

The one exception where younger children outperform older learners in a second language is in the area of pronunciation. Younger children acquire native-like pronunciation faster than older learners (McLaughlin 1992). As educators, we should respect that learning English as a second language is as difficult for children in our classrooms as it would be for us to acquire native-like proficiency in an additional language as an adult.

We have much to teach our CLDLs. Learning both language and content requires a high cognitive demand. This is true for English language learners as well as English-only school English learners (SELs). It can even be more difficult for young children because they do not have access to the memory techniques and other strategies that more experienced learners may use in acquiring vocabulary and in learning the grammatical rules of the language (McLaughlin 1992). Explicit instruction is essential. Do not assume that once children are able to converse comfortably in English, they are in full control of the language. For school-aged children, there is much more involved in learning a second language than just learning how to speak it. A child who is proficient in face-to-face communication (BICS), has not necessarily achieved proficiency in the more abstract and noncontext-based academic language (CALP) needed to engage in many classroom activities. The gap between BICS and CALP is even more pronounced in the higher grades.

Consider that a student who is learning a second language might be having language problems in reading and writing which might not be readily apparent if the student's oral abilities are used as the measure of English proficiency. For students from minority language backgrounds, many of their problems in reading and writing at the middle and highschool levels stem from limitations in vocabulary and syntactic knowledge in the second language. Even students who are skilled orally can have a large BICS-CALP gap.

One component of the BICS-CALP gap is learning rate. Not all students learn in the same way or at the same rate. There are two issues here. The first issue relates to differences among CLDL groups. The second issue relates to differences among learners within each culturally and linguistically diverse group. Research indicates that children from mainstream middle and higher socioeconomic status American families have different ways of talking. Mainstream children are accustomed to an analytic style, in which the truth of specific arguments is deduced from general propositions. Many children from culturally diverse groups are accustomed to an inductive style of talking in which fundamental assumptions must be inferred from a series of concrete statements. Children from mainstream families are rewarded for clear and logical thinking. Culturally and linguistically diverse learners who enter school accustomed to using language in a divergent way from what is expected in school will experience tension and frustration (McLaughlin 1992).

Another component of the BICS-CALP gap is academic development. Here, we consider all schoolwork in every subject matter, and at each grade level. With each grade advancement, academic knowledge and conceptual development transfers from the first language to the second language. Students with high language proficiency in L1 and CALP in L1 are likely to have a smaller BICS-CALP gap in English. They have more in their L1 lexicon and L1 schema on which to hang new learning. The final component of the BICS-CALP gap is the cognitive dimension. Until recently, this area has been largely neglected by American second-language educators. Language teaching was always simplified, structured, and sequenced. Unfortunately, this approach diminished academic content to cognitively undemanding tasks. Too often, English language development neglected the crucial role of cognitive academic development in either language. Thus, while BICS developed, largely from the increased and enhanced social aspects of the classroom, CALP experienced retarded growth. The BICS-CALP gap can be effectively and efficiently closed through a CA-RTI implementation. Research evidences that English language learners who start school with serious delays can make substantial improvements in reading when provided with scientifically-based reading and researched instruction (Kamps et al. 2007; Quiroga et al. 2002).

Conclusion

This chapter examined a brief history of ELD instruction and made the case for the harmony that must exist between instructing for cultural appropriateness, increasing students' basic interpersonal communication skills (BICS) and increasing cognitive academic language proficiency (CALP). CA-RTI implementation must provide harmony between the cultural and the cognitive aspects of instruction, eliminating the BICS-CALP gap.

Reflect and Act

1. Examine your lesson plans for introducing new vocabulary. Focus on the words your students need to know, not just the ones identified in the text. Use the vocabulary chart from (figure 7.2) below to craft the teaching and assessment of those words.

Fig. 7.2. Identify Vocabulary

Tier 2 Words (Text Selection Specific)	Tier 3 Words (Content Specific)

2. After conducting a vocabulary lesson, write a quick reflection, even if it is just on a sticky note. Note what worked, what did not work, and how you can refine the instruction for a future lesson.

Chapter 8

Don't Leave Anything about Teaching and Learning to Chance

Regardless of their competency in BICS or CALP, all children can learn. All children respond to feedback, appropriate or otherwise. We must remove the element of chance from learning through instructional methodology, feedback, and praise. First we offer an overview of theories of learning. Then we will look at three strategies, or methodologies, of classroom instruction with a strong emphasis on achieving true learning for CLDLs, particularly in Tier 3. Finally, we offer a Theory to Practice activity to provide you with some tools to implement immediately.

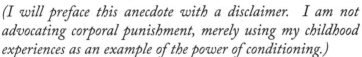

Practitioner's Perspective

(I will preface this anecdote with a disclaimer. I am not advocating corporal punishment, merely using my childhood experiences as an example of the power of conditioning.)

In the disciplinary model my mother and our community used, conditioning had a great deal to do with my learned behavior. I grew up at a time when people besides your parents had permission to discipline you for misbehaving. The concept of a village raising a child was not an idea, but rather a fact of life. In church, we knew whom to sit next to: those aunties, biological or adopted, who would overlook your indiscretions. We also knew whom to avoid: those less tolerant, who could keep you in line with just a glance. If fate left you sitting next to one of the latter, your behavior was suddenly very carefully self-monitored. As I approached adolescence, fear of punishment still worked on my thought processes, until I finally learned to override that fear. Conditioning still has a great influence on learning, though.

When thinking about how children learn, many questions come to mind. How much of our development relates to genetics? to environment? to culture? to our experiences? Does socioeconomic status affect our potential? In 1959, Dorothy Law published the first version of her poem, "Children Learn What They Live." The poem has undergone multiple revisions over the years, but the premise remains the same: children learn vicariously. In the classroom, instruction must address both social and cognitive competence. CA-RTI implementation misses the mark if the social and emotional or cultural aspect of instruction is lost.

Much evidence supports this premise. The National Education Goals Panel suggested that promoting the social and cognitive competence of all students is central to accomplishing U. S. national education goals (2000). Several researchers have found that establishing comprehensive school-based programs to facilitate academic and socio-emotional development reduces behavior problems and associated deleterious outcomes (Lewis, Sugai, and Colvin 1999; Roeser 2001; Roeser and Eccles 2000). For instance, a good reading program can prevent discipline problems that stem from frustration and failure; a good social-behavioral, mental wellness program can improve reading achievement by increasing instructional time (Skinner and Smith 1992). Together, an effective reading program and effective social skills program can significantly increase the learning and adjustment of children (Slavin and Fashola 1998). Research supports multiple aspects of the CA-RTI model.

Learning encompasses numerous factors and variables. Each student starts school with his or her own unique experiences from birth. Every day, the interactions with others, in and out of the classroom, affect their social and cognitive development. Their response to instruction is impacted by the information we provide them, the values and morés of their many cultures, where they live, and more. We cannot account for life experiences that affect students' views of the material they must learn. As educators, we must simply recognize that each child is a unique individual.

While some commonalities may exist by gender, socioeconomic status, innate intelligence levels, culture, and so on, the bottom line is each child's learning experiences will be different. Since governing authorities determine the standards to which teaching and learning must adhere, we have to consider how best to approach teaching and learning for our CLDLs.

Practitioner's Perspective

When I taught in a low-performing school filled with students at high risk of failure, those students with lower performances were more likely to act on their emotions than those who showed higher performance levels. Was this learned behavior? Quite likely it was. In many at-risk populations, one of the most commonly learned behaviors is escape. These students are the victims of the soft bigotry of low expectations and dysteachia. Students who have been taught over the course of six, seven, or even 10 years in school that they cannot read, cannot learn, actually learn quite a bit. They learn that misbehavior provides an escape from the classroom environment where they know only failure. Put it this way: if a child lives with low expectations, he or she learns to not bother learning.

Review of Theories of Learning

Chapter 2 introduced the concept of *dysteachia* in reference to the instructional acts that make learning difficult to impossible for culturally and linguistically diverse learners. To eliminate dysteachia, we must lower the affective filter and provide students with academic instruction that is not only cognitively appropriate, but academically appropriate as well. After many repeated successes, we extinguish the misbehavior, and students have greater learning opportunities. Eventually, with accelerated instruction through the CA-RTI model, students come to perform at or near grade level, experience daily success in most if not all classrooms, and no longer act out. What theories of learning support this hypothesis? Theories of learning can be generally classified as either environmental or epigenetic theories (although one, social cognitive theory, is a blend of the two). Environmental or nurture theories are also known as continuous development theories or behaviorist theories. They emphasize the role of the environment in molding behavior. According to nurture theory, learning involves the acquisition of abilities that are not innate, but rather reliant on environmental feedback. Epigenetic or nature theories encompass all the "stage" theories of development: people pass through stages in life, predetermined by genetics. At each stage there are crises or critical issues to be resolved. Since educators have no control over genetics, we will focus on environmental theories for the purpose of intervention.

Environmental Theories

Behaviorist

Behaviorist theory as developed by Watson (1930) explains learning by emphasizing observable changes in behavior. Behaviorism defines learning as *conditioning*. Watson's classical conditioning is the explanation of learning through association. Watson felt that conditioning was the only variable responsible for development and learning. All behavior is the result of experience and environment. Learned behavior is reflexive: associating a previously neutral stimulus with an unconditioned stimulus will evoke a conditioned response. True behaviorism is all about nurturing. Watson wrote:

"Give me a dozen healthy infants, well-formed, and my own specified world to bring them up in and I'll guarantee to take any one at random and train him to become any type of specialist I might select—doctor, lawyer, artist, merchant-chief and, yes, even beggar-man and thief, regardless of his talents, penchants, tendencies, abilities, vocations, and race of his ancestors" (1930).

Classical Conditioning

Classical conditioning is most commonly associated with the works of Edward Thorndike and B. F. Skinner. Classical conditioning is an explanation of learning that emphasizes observable changes in behavior. It states that learning is operant; therefore, what students learn is based on the consequences of their behavior. A negative consequence is not necessarily a punishment, but can be viewed as an opportunity to learn.

Humanism

Humanism theory as developed by Abraham Maslow is an explanation of learning that focuses on children's physiological needs, attitudes, and feelings. Maslow taught that there was a Hierarchy of Needs, and that human behavior can be explained by the individual's motivation to satisfy those needs. He believed that a healthy child in the course of normal development will choose what is good for him or herself given a full range of choices. The hierarchy was based on (from lowest to highest) physiological needs, safety needs, love and belonging, esteem, and self-actualization. In order for higher needs, such as esteem and self-actualization, to be sought, lower level needs had to be satisfied. Sometimes students come to school and do almost nothing day after day. You might wonder why they even bother coming to school. Consider this: the classroom might be the place that best meets their needs.

Social Cognitive Theory

There is nothing wrong with the students. There is something wrong with the approach to instruction that results in students not learning. That something is *dysteachia*. The success of the CA-RTI model leans heavily on social cognitive or social learning theories (Griffin 1991). Social cognitive theory emphasizes both environmental influences and cognition in development. Social cognitive theory bridges nature and nurture. Bandura theorized that children are partly responsible for creating their own environments based on their behavior. Individuals do not passively accept their environments, but rather work to shape and control them through action and reaction. Bandura described four phases of observational learning that occurred constantly as new information was presented: attention, retention, reproduction, and motivation. According to Bandura, students learn by observing modeled behavior in the attention and retention phases, and imitate those behaviors through the reproduction phase. Learning is reinforced vicariously during the motivation phase. In the absence of adult feedback, students will adjust their own behavior by observing the consequences of their own and others' behaviors. Bandura theorized that not only did environment shape behavior, but that behavior also shaped the environment. This became a concept which is now known as *reciprocal determinism* (Bandura 1991). He later added the additional factor of psychological processes: the ability of humans to hold images and language in memory as a method of learning.

Fig. 8.1. Five Phases of Social Cognitive Theory

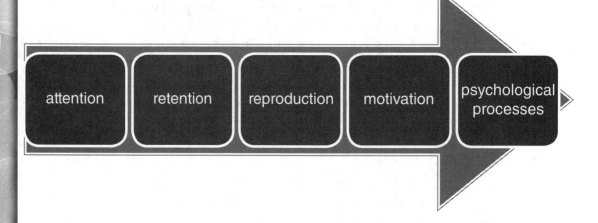

Social cognitive theory puts the student in a position of always being successful. It accounts for both the student's intrinsic ability (nature), and the effects of good teaching (nurture). (See figure 8.2.)

Fig. 8.2. Social Cognitive Theory

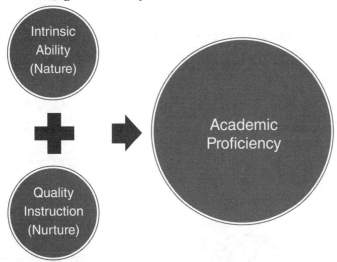

It requires that both curriculum and instruction consider the big picture concepts that must be learned and that the information be delivered in the incremental, sequential pieces that allow the student to learn, synthesize, and evaluate. Students are able to build new constructs from prior knowledge.

Social cognitive theory allows a symbiotic relationship between teaching and learning, and strengthens the skills of both parties involved. The CA-RTI model requires that quality instruction consider and address each student's intrinsic abilities and then build towards proficiency within two years. Social cognitive theory encompasses both the behavioral and academic domains of learning, suggesting four implications for classroom implementation:

- Provide specific praise that enables and supports students to take personal responsibility for success and failure.

- Validate student interests and help them make connections between the instruction and their world.

- Move from providing extrinsic rewards to developing intrinsic motivation as quickly as possible.

- Facilitate the growth of behavioral self-monitoring.

Model Strategies That Develop Students' Metacognition

The strategies of cooperative learning (Slavin 2005), reciprocal teaching (Palincsar and Brown 1984), and direct instruction (Engelmann 2008) are all built on social cognitive theory, and span the spectrum of implicit to explicit instruction (figure 8.3).

We will examine each of these strategies and look at their correlation to the five phases of social cognitive theory (figure 8.1) and curriculum design.

Fig. 8.3. Implicit to Explicit Instruction

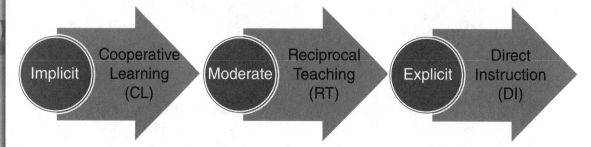

Cooperative Learning

At the implicit end of the spectrum, cooperative learning models have students work in heterogeneous groups of four to six students. The students themselves take responsibility for investigations that lead to learning academic material. Cooperative learning exemplifies a most implicit strategy. Generally, the groups receive rewards (grades) based on the amount all members of the group have learned. The idea behind this method is that when groups receive rewards (rather than individuals), students become motivated to help one another master academic materials. Many proponents of cooperative learning believe that the variety among members provides models of behavior that surface at various points throughout the process. In cooperative learning, the students themselves model behavior and learning for one another.

There is a place for cooperative learning in the CA-RTI model. However, that place is not in the instruction of critical material for students needing Tier 2 or Tier 3 instruction. In the CA-RTI model, cooperative learning must remain at Tier 1, for students with no risk of failure. Why? Examine cooperative learning in relation to the five phases of social cognitive theory.

The first phase in social cognitive theory is attention. In cooperative learning, early discussion and brainstorming make up the attention phase. There may be one member of the group whose personality lends them towards leadership, a skill which may be observed by other members of the group and, in phase two, retained. The retention of these behaviors may be practiced within the group or simply kept within the observer's mind. The memory may lie dormant until the learner faces a situation where he or she must reproduce the behavior. Within the cooperative learning group, no reinforcement may be present; however, motivation may come in the form of reciprocal determination. The idea behind reciprocal determination is that the student impacts his or her environment as well as the cooperative group through participation and effort. The learning group shapes the learner as well. It is almost like a snowball effect. The more the learner participates, the more others in the group participate. As the group develops synergy, intrinsic motivation is fueled and a desire for the group to do well also develops. As members of the group first interact, some external motivation may be required to initiate cooperation.

Cooperative learning is effective for developing BICS, but what about CALP? What happens to the CLDL who has no schema for the subject or a divergent schema that does not map to the mainstream? What happens to learning when the behaviors exhibited within the group do not reflect the expected norms? For students at-risk, the cooperative learning method leaves too much to chance. This is a gamble our CLDLs cannot afford.

Reciprocal Teaching

Midway across the spectrum between implicit and explicit, reciprocal teaching combines both teacher-led and student-led instruction. Reciprocal teaching was designed to teach metacognitive skills. Reciprocal teaching uses instruction and teacher modeling to improve the reading performance of students who have poor comprehension.

Initially removed from the student, reciprocal teaching requires the teacher to model the strategy to be learned. While first designed and implemented in underperforming settings, this model has now been commonly applied to the instructional framework of most basal reading programs.

There is a place for reciprocal teaching in the CA-RTI model. That place is primarily Tier 1 and Tier 2 instruction. With rigor, it may be used in the latter part of the reproduction phase in Tier 3. Reciprocal teaching is a tool for comprehension. For students at-risk who are not decoding with fluency to automaticity, our primary focus must be on building the decoding skills. Remember, students who cannot decode with fluency have little cognitive energy left for comprehension. (Refer to Chapter 2 for a thorough discussion of that topic.) Why? Look at reciprocal teaching within the five phases of social cognitive theory.

Attention comes from engaging the student in text. Reciprocal teaching supports retention by having students practice the behavior they have seen modeled. Reciprocal teaching calls for reproduction as a necessary component of the instruction. Through interaction, once again we see the dynamic of reciprocal determination taking place, as the learner reproduces the modeled behavior and receives feedback. Over time, students take on more of the responsibility for reciprocal teaching, moving into the fifth phase of psychological processes.

Reciprocal teaching works towards the development of both BICS and CALP. Reciprocal teaching provides the teacher the opportunity to front-load where necessary and intervene when necessary so that CLDLs make appropriate connections. But two limitations to reciprocal teaching exist for students in Tier 3. First, instructional time is constrained. Students in Tier 3 need as much time as possible with accelerated instruction. Reciprocal teaching allows for time on-task to diminish as instruction is handed over to the learners in the latter phases. Second, reciprocal teaching is designed to teach only one component of reading—comprehension (although it has been successfully put into practice in mathematics problem solving).

Direct Instruction

At the explicit end of the spectrum lies direct instruction, specifically Engelmann's (2008) model of instruction. Engelmann's operating premise is that "the teacher is responsible for the learning of the children" (2008); not just some children, but every child. Direct instruction explicitly reflects social cognitive learning across all five phases. Much of the research on direct instruction has focused on economically disadvantaged and culturally diverse children. To that end, it has been more thoroughly validated for the CLDL population in the CA-RTI model. Reflect on the connection to the five phases of Social Cognitive Theory.

For the attention phase, direct instruction programs rely on fast-paced, highly engaging academic instruction designed to keep students focused on the task at hand. Beginning with explicit explanations and teacher models, students know exactly what is expected both behaviorally and cognitively. Attention is facilitated through consistent formats of instruction that build and then work within students' existing schema. Retention is aided by reducing the amount of newly introduced information in each lesson. Direct instruction lessons typically include approximately 30% new information and 70% review information. Students constantly refresh and reorder their existing knowledge while increasing their knowledge base. (This reflects the concept of massed and distributed practice from Chapter 6.) Through modeling and explicitly teaching higher-ordered comprehension, students will learn to generalize and broaden their understanding.

The reproduction phase is supported through guided practice. Where students are likely to make mistakes, more guided practice is provided. Students receive specific feedback throughout the lesson. It is the teacher's task in direct instruction to deliver explicit feedback informing students of what was correct and incorrect, both behaviorally and academically. The teacher provides extrinsic motivation through praise and some type of point or reward system. Daily success leads to intrinsic motivation. Finally, a high level of interaction exists between students and teachers. Psychological processes develop through this interaction as students learn and hold on to the language of instruction and learning. Later, students have the language and the generalization skills to support their learning in other areas.

Direct instruction not only develops both BICS and CALP, but it does so in a readily observable and routinely measurable fashion. This is ideal. Direct instruction is designed for homogeneous groups, which makes it quite suitable for Tier 3 instruction. Direct instruction provides structured front-loading for each concept and targeted intervention and scaffolding so that CLDLs do not have an opportunity to fail.

Students in Tier 3 need as much time as possible with accelerated instruction, and direct instruction maintains a strong time-on-task component. Finally, direct instruction has been validated for instruction in all domains of English language arts and mathematics. (For a comprehensive meta-analysis of the efficacy of direct instruction methodology for CLDLs at risk, see the study by Borman et al. [2002] on comprehensive school reform and student achievement.)

Reaching Critical Mass on Feedback

It is important to provide proper feedback so that students benefit and correct mistakes. Corrections instruct and support learning. Self-esteem improves when students know that they can read, write, and calculate. Feedback does more than correct; it supports appropriate social and cognitive performance. The two branches of feedback, behavioral and academic, each contain praise and corrections. (See figure 8.4.).

However, consider keeping praise separate. Error correction is vital. Teachers must correct every error they hear from a student during instruction. This is critical in teaching reading and mathematics. Students must not only know when they have erred, they must also be told what the error was, and what is the correct response.

Fig. 8.4. Direct Instruction

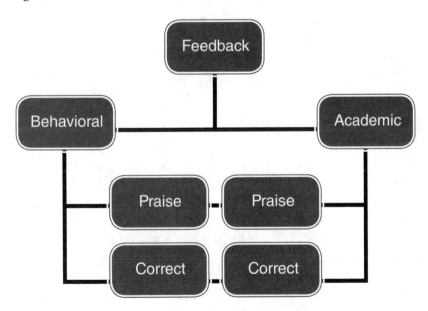

Practitioner's Perspective

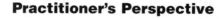

Growing up, my mother was known as the Grammar Monitor. Sure, it was an annoyance as a child, but a blessing in adult professional life. So, when I was told in teacher training that I should never correct the language of an English language learner, I suffered extreme cognitive dissonance. How will students ever learn correct grammar, language, and syntax if we do not provide corrections?

One of my earliest teaching assignments was in a school district that allowed "creative spelling" through grade six, with no corrections allowed! I immediately knew I was in the wrong place. As a sixth-grade teacher years later, I taught sentence diagramming to all my students. I was a rebel with a cause. Some of my colleagues thought I was crazy. My CLDLs, all of whom were at risk, loved it. The feedback from the students buffeted my resolve to teach explicit, meaningful grammar, usage, and mechanics. My CLDLs spoke better, wrote better, and asked for clarification when things did not make sense. They asked for daily lessons in diagramming sentences.

In a study conducted by Gersten, Carnine, and Williams (1982) they examined the effect of varied feedback in passage-reading tasks. Two groups of 13 beginning readers read the same passage a total of three times. On the second and third readings, one group received feedback on errors. The other group received no feedback on errors for the second and third readings. The feedback group improved from the first to the third reading, with errors dropping from 4% to 0.7%. However, the errors for the no-feedback group increased from 3% to 5.4%. The results of this study show that corrective feedback is critical.

I do not support verbally berating error-makers. Look at this example of an appropriate academic error correction:

> **Teacher:** Look at the sentence, "The sporty red car went racing down the highway."
>
> **Student:** The spotty...
>
> **Teacher** *(interrupting immediately after "spotty")*: Stop. That word is *sporty*. What is the word?
>
> **Student:** Sporty.
>
> **Teacher:** Yes. Go back and read the sentence again.

And here is an example of an inappropriate academic error correction:

> **Teacher:** Look at the sentence, "The sporty red car went racing down the highway."
>
> **Student:** The spotty...
>
> **Teacher:** Oh my goodness! Didn't I teach you that word yesterday? Where is your head? Are you even trying? I don't know what I'm going to do with you! Someone else read, please?"

In the second scenario, the student will stop listening to the rest of the lesson. Instead, he or she will count the minutes until recess, or worse, express his or her frustration in a destructive way.

Error correction must be supported with praise—lots and lots of praise. In fact, the recommended ratio of praise to corrections is 9:1 (Marchand-Martella, Slocum, and Martella 2004). For every error correction, the teacher should provide nine praises for correct academic responses. Here is an example (continuing from above):

> **Student** *(re-reads)*: The sporty red car went racing down the highway.

> **Teacher:** Excellent job reading that sentence!

Now the teacher needs to provide eight more comments of praise before another student makes an error. That is a lot of praise. This is why instruction in Tier 1 needs to be targeted towards student ability. If students cannot perform in the curriculum, teachers will spend all of their time correcting, and students will be frustrated. Students in Tier 2 and Tier 3 need to hear praise for what they do correctly. Students who have experienced prolonged failure may not know correct from incorrect behavior because they have not been shown.

Behavioral feedback requires the same 9:1 ratio of praise to corrections. This requires the teacher to establish behavioral expectations and then stick to them.

Practitioner's Perspective

Here is an example of how to set up expectations and include praise at the same time (adapted from my own opening statements to my secondary students):

Ladies and gentlemen, we have a lot of work to do in a short 55 minutes each day, so here are my expectations for getting started. Each day when you enter the room you will remove your hats and hoods. Thank you for being courteous. You will pull up any sagging pants. Thank you for showing respect for our dress code. You will pick up your numbered books and workbooks from the materials shelf for this class period. Thank you for remembering your student number. You will take your materials to your desk, place your backpack underneath your desk, and keep all aisles and the backs of your chairs clear. Thank you for creating safe walking spaces. You will take out your pencil, your red pen for correcting, and your blue pen. Thank you for having all of your materials. You will open your book and your workbook to the lesson for the day as noted on the board. Thank you for being ready to learn. We will all be ready for class to begin within two minutes of the bell. Why? Because you are all on your way to becoming world-class learners!

Students do not need this speech every day, but consider reiterating the expectations for the first three to 10 days of class. Usually, if the students can recite the expectations by heart, you will be able to stop repeating them. They will have reached the fifth phase of social cognitive learning—psychological processes. At this stage, they hold the language in long-term memory and can pull it out when needed. It takes about one minute to deliver that speech. In that time, students receive seven behavioral expectations and seven specific behavioral praises. Think about other expectations you need to explicitly tell to your students.

Make the expectations clear, consistent, specific, and explicit. Have no more than five so the children can learn them easily and quickly. Most importantly, have one generic rule to cover all bases. My generic rule is, "Respect others." Those two little words can cover a myriad of unanticipated negative behaviors.

. . . .

Theory to Practice Activity

One of the greatest challenges of providing corrective feedback is developing a repertoire of phrases that roll right off the tongue. Keep a set of Praise Phrase sticky notes to help you provide positive feedback, no matter what material you are teaching. Refer to the Praise Phrase sticky notes until you are able to retrain your brain and improve your repertoire enough that you can offer authentic praise with automaticity and generosity.

Start with several 3"x 3" sticky notes and write as many Praise Phrase stems as you can. Then, practice using them during instruction.

Figure 8.5 offers a few suggestions to get you started:

Fig. 8.5. Praise Stems for Feedback

I like the way you...

Excellent job...

You showed skill in...

Nice way to remember...

Good job showing how to...

. . . .

For some students, a model of instruction that constantly praises appropriate responses and behaviors provides more information in one hour than they would typically receive about their learning in an entire day. Through a routine and consistent process, the learner easily internalizes the social and cognitive behaviors that promote success in the classroom. The students themselves become the standard of behavior and models for others in the classroom, especially new learners, to follow.

Make Connections and Check Your Mindset

Do you agree or disagree with the statements below?

1. A clear explanation is easier to understand than an ambiguous statement.

2. You learn less when you have an overload of information.

3. Guided practice helps when you are likely to make mistakes.

4. Appropriate practice improves your performance.

5. You learn more when you are actively involved.

I have never had an educator disagree with any of these statements. Now, connect Social Cognitive Theory to these five statements. Layer on cooperative learning, reciprocal teaching, and direct instruction. Finally, consider the CA-RTI model. Figure 8.6 now represents the picture of ideal instruction for CLDLs.

Fig. 8.6. Ideal Instruction for CLDLs

Attention: provide clear, consistent instruction

Retention: avoid an overload of information

Reproduction: guide practice to mastery

Motivation: provide positive praise, explicit feedback

Psychological Processes: transferable skills

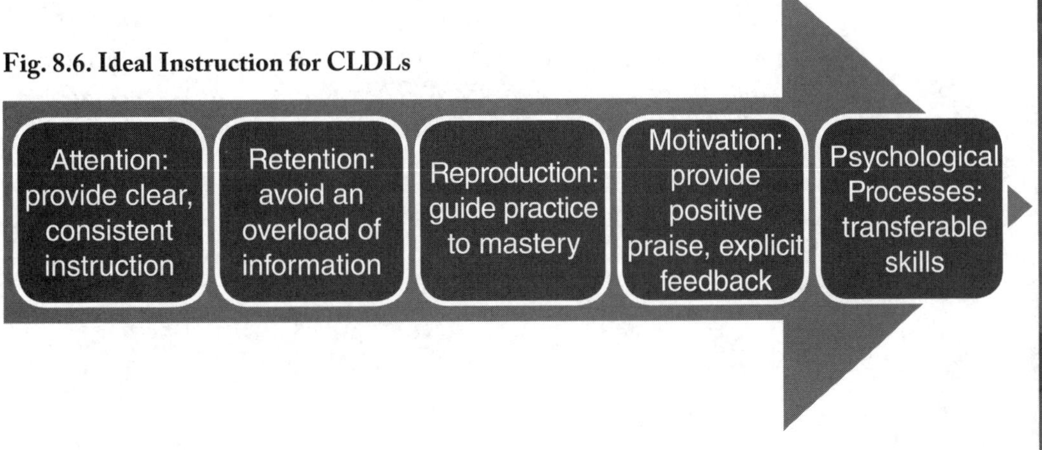

Review the graphics for the CA-RTI model presented in Chapter 3 (figures 3.2 and 3.3, p. 50). Sketch them out on a large sheet of paper. In each box or circle, fill in the appropriate instructional method for each tier. Consider the BICS-CALP gap and the necessary teaching and learning for your CLDLs. Which of your students, particularly your CLDLs, can afford to miss out on one or more of the five phases of social cognitive learning?

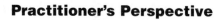

Practitioner's Perspective

I always chuckle when I recall my first real teaching assignment. The permanent teacher for a seventh grade science class had walked out one day, never to return. The students had dealt with 30 substitutes in as many instructional days. Before the end of my first day as the substitute, I was hired for a long-term position.

Evidently, the students in this particular series of classes, especially fifth period, were a bit challenging (at least that was the expectation and belief of the faculty). No other substitute before had lasted through fifth period without the assistance of an administrator. Yet, for some reason, when the principal arrived on my watch, he entered a well-ordered, completely controlled classroom. I was hired immediately after school.

There was nothing wrong with those students. They had clearly learned their behavioral limits from their instructors. Then, they met me. I came in with clearly articulated high expectations, and explicitly defined consequences for appropriate and inappropriate behavior. The result was an immediate, observable change in behavior.

Conclusion

In this age of accountability, curriculum choice centers on standards to determine exactly what children must learn, in what sequence it should be taught, and to what level it must be mastered. Effective CA-RTI will accomplish all of that, and will also deliver on the promise of producing students who are able to master the concepts. In the 21st century school, social cognitive learning as the basis for curriculum design and delivery makes good on that promise with consistency through persistent, dedicated, and focused delivery of content to the children most at risk for failure.

As educators, we must remove the element of chance from learning. The more we use positive environmental elements to increase human potential, the greater the results. Ethnicity has nothing whatsoever to do with human intellectual potential. However, cultural diversity does play a role. The more divergent a student's home culture from the culture of school, the harder we must work to ensure that the student learns the culture of school to experience success. Moreover, socioeconomic status has a tremendous impact on potential (Hart and Risley 1995). We reviewed three theories of learning very pertinent to the CA-RTI model. These theories were layered onto the CA-RTI model with a strong emphasis on achieving best possible outcomes for CLDLs in Tier 3 intervention. When it comes to creating successful CLDLs, we cannot leave anything about teaching and learning to chance.

Reflect and Act

Work with a colleague, and be ready to open up some tough dialogue in these areas:

1. Create your own Praise Phrase sticky note and put it somewhere in your classroom where you will see it all day during instruction. Share your comments with your colleagues, and ask for suggestions from them, as well.

2. Give your students two behavioral expectations and two academic expectations at the beginning of a reading or math lesson. Use the stems on your sticky note to provide tons of praise. Record in a journal the phrases that were the most effective for students.

Chapter 9

Getting from Where We Are to Where We Need to Be

"Would you tell me please, which way I ought to go from here?" asked Alice. "That depends a good deal on where you want to get to" said the Cat. "I don't much care where—" said Alice. "Then it doesn't matter which way you go," said the Cat. "—so long as I get somewhere," Alice added as an explanation.

This excerpt from Lewis Carroll's *Alice in Wonderland* (1865) gives us a nice context for the work of the professional learning community, professional development, and the development of your CA-RTI plan. When it comes to providing a rigorous CA-RTI model, unlike Alice, you must have a plan for all the components of the model. If the CA-RTI plan does not specifically address where students are to go in terms of growth, gap closure, and benchmarks, you cannot know if you spent your time in the right endeavors. In retrospect, a school may or may not see growth. The plan for both students and teachers is designed to help get the school from one place to another within a reasonable amount of time.

To navigate, you must plan for both a professional learning community and professional development. You need to chart a course for both restructuring and reculturing. Most importantly, you will have to do the right things, correctly, and often enough to make a difference. Stay the course; the results will come.

Now you can think about putting all the pieces together and turning them into practice. You cannot have a CA-RTI implementation without a professional learning community. Here is how to make that happen.

Creating a Professional Learning Community: It Takes a Village

Also referred to as communities of practice, the professional learning community (PLC) holds key responsibilities in the CA-RTI model. The PLC must be created in order for the school or district as a whole to gain skill in three areas. The primary focus of the PLC lies in creating knowledge through collaboration with key stakeholders. Secondly, the PLC should work to acquire knowledge from others, such as staff developers and experts. Finally, the PLC must work to transfer that knowledge both within the school or district and throughout the community of stakeholders. In the implementation of a CA-RTI model, schools and districts must do the following:

- plan for implementation

- professionally develop all educators

- articulate goals and outcomes

- align curriculum and instruction from grade to grade and school to school.

In order to provide a cohesive school-to-school alignment that supports the CLDL, the CA-RTI curriculum must support high standards, rigor, and strong instructional methods for CLDLs at all three tiers. To provide this level of integrated support and development requires a community of educators focused on the educational goals of the students: a professional learning community. The research on professional learning communities is still in its infancy; however, the structuring and evidence of efficacy is well supported. Schools and districts are often quite proficient at restructuring. It is performed with relative frequency, but to what end? The agreed-upon goals and outcomes, timetables and programs look great on paper, but are often discarded due to some unforeseen or unseen element. A change in administration, a new curriculum adoption, high teacher turnover, or impatience may lead to abandonment. To make CA-RTI effective, schools must go beyond restructuring to reculturing. Reculturing makes the true change difference. Fullan's (2000) premise supports the synergistic relationship between teaching and outcomes in a collaborative school or district. The two feed upon each other. This synergy results in improved teaching, learning, and thus assessment outcomes.

Reculturing comprises a big part of the development of PLCs. In a recultured school, the focus on outcomes extends well beyond the annual review of high-stakes test scores and the intense focus of test preparation. PLCs in recultured schools concentrate on pedagogy and outcomes consistently throughout the year. The earlier discussions of RTI (Chapter 3) and the assessment cycle (Chapter 4) provide a roadmap for consistently reviewing the effects of pedagogy through tiered curriculum implementation and multiple assessments. A team of stakeholders must regularly examine the data at each school. In a district-wide PLC, individuals from each school should serve as representatives to the broader body.

Sometimes the organizational structure of a school or district may view PLC teams as treading on the turf of others. Beware of roadblocks and pitfalls; know what they are, and work to eliminate them. Collaboration serves to modify or change the behavior of stakeholders so that new knowledge and insights replace the old mindset. We cannot change the culture of our students' homes. We can change only the culture of the school to serve in the best interest of the CLDL, and all learners.

Over the years, many lessons have been learned in implementing broad-scale curricular changes, particularly in the instance of RTI-like models. There is no need to reinvent a perfectly functioning wheel. To get

Check Yourself

- Do I have time to address pedagogy and assessment?

- How often each week (or month) does my team review achievement data?

- How often do we review what works (or not) in the present curriculum?

- What pitfalls and road-blocks can I anticipate? How can we overcome these?

your PLC started, or to improve upon the one you already have in a way that supports CA-RTI implementation, take into consideration the following:

1. Both school and central office administrators, need a foundational understanding of the CA-RTI model. They must be familiar with the various curricula to be implemented at each tier, and the advantages of the curricular choices made to address the needs of CLDLs in the CA-RTI model.

2. Administrators have a responsibility to carefully evaluate the adjustments needed in order to effectively implement the CA-RTI model with fidelity. This may require the guidance of a trained CA-RTI implementation specialist. In addition, pre-implementation professional development for teachers, paraprofessionals, counselors, school psychologists, administrators, and parents is requisite.

Remember, a PLC is not workshop-driven professional development. The work of the PLC never ends. Plan for ongoing site-based professional development provided by experts in their fields. Site-based professional development should reflect the needs of the school. It may support a particular curriculum, language acquisition, culture, assessment data—the list is comprehensive to say the least. As you plan for this, do not neglect to plan for a timely takeover. Remember, while the second job of the PLC is working to acquire knowledge from others, such as staff developers and experts, the PLC must also work to transfer that knowledge both within the school or district and throughout the community of stakeholders. That requires an emphasis on building internal capacity.

Professional Development

More important than having a *plan* for professional development is actually achieving successful professional development. This should be an ongoing process that gives power to groups and individuals in the instructional setting, the organization as a whole, curriculum, instruction, and assessment so that students experience targeted academic and social development. Most of us have heard the pundits cite studies and data that poor and minority students have the least access to high-quality teachers and instruction. Unfortunately, the data cannot be refuted. Much work remains to close the achievement gap that exists with CLDLs. To close that gap will take hard work by highly qualified and motivated teachers.

Many models exist for professional development in the K–12 public schools. Some models work, others do not. Some designs focus on developing the teacher in isolation from the student population with which they work. They focus on the general art of teaching. This is not good for CLDLs. Research on teaching and learning has deepened our collective knowledge on the subject of reaching and teaching the CLDL. For the CA-RTI model to be effective, the PLC professional development team must take a more targeted approach to professional development.

In general, large school districts model professional development opportunities on a career continuum approach, where participants move from instruction in a broad variety of content areas to more concentrated learning in specific topics chosen by the teachers. Most plans reflect only the number of hours required by negotiated contracts with the teachers' unions. Typical courses include special education and mainstreaming, English language learner support, content-area tips and techniques, technology, classroom management, and whole-school reform to increase accountability. It is rare to see a comprehensive, targeted plan for developing teaching professionals over a period of more than one year with a goal of improving teaching and learning for the students in that particular district. However, this may be just what the doctor ordered.

Practitioner's Perspective

As a coach for a large urban school district in the Midwest, I worked with reading coaches on the challenges they faced with English language learners. There was nothing wrong with the children. There was much language diversity, though. Because the influx of English language learners was new to the state, they had no English language development coursework requirement for standard teaching certificates. The district could have easily continued providing professional development, but that was not the most pressing issue for this district. The real issue revolved around the specific challenges of teaching reading to CLDLs, including linguistic and cultural aspects. With a targeted approach, we addressed both. Coursework was developed for coaches to learn about language acquisition, how to teach English to English language learners, how to teach reading to English language learners, and the connections between language learning and reading development. The standard fare just would not have worked.

Successful professional development supports the transfer of information to actual practice so that students are the true beneficiaries. Teachers must know the justification for using specific teaching methods and why fidelity to those methods is requisite to the success of program for both students and teachers (Brady and Moats 1997; Gersten et al. 2005). Several chapters in this book were devoted to appropriate instruction in each tier and the use of validated methodologies for the learners in each tier. But curriculum cannot deliver as promised without appropriate delivery. When educators follow a validated method with fidelity, they provide the appropriate foundation for differentiation (Gersten et al. 2005). What is the point of differentiating for students if the method of core instruction or the delivery is flawed, particularly if differentiation follows on the same flawed practices?

Professional development is not only necessary for curriculum and instruction, but also for understanding how and why to work together collaboratively to achieve the outcomes desired from the CA-RTI implementation. Start with a needs assessment to determine the professional development needed for all stakeholders: teachers, support staff, administrators, leaders, and the broader school community, including parents.

Base Ongoing Professional Development on Effective Strategies

Not all instructional practices are valid, no matter how much fun they are to implement. Exposure to the curriculum is not enough. We cannot allow practitioners to close their doors and teach according to their own philosophies and desires if evidence shows that their actions are ineffective, and in the long run, harmful. Undoubtedly, the rigor of a firm CA-RTI implementation has caused many teachers to react with strong aversion to implementation with fidelity. That is why a strong professional development and coaching model is vital for every implementation.

A multidimensional ongoing professional development model is a bit like a CA-RTI model. Begin with a baseline and develop a trajectory of learning outcomes. Teachers will naturally be at different levels in terms of their instructional expertise. Perhaps their levels reflect their educational background. Perhaps there exists a pedagogical philosophy not in keeping with the scientific findings on instruction. Or possibly, there are other barriers such as language or culture. Your needs assessment may reveal interesting data in this regard.

Just like the CA-RTI model, professional development needs some progress monitoring checkpoints and some benchmarking periods with goals that must be met. Classroom data will provide evidence as to how things are really working in practice. As the PLC team works on the professional development plan, consider the need for weekly and monthly meetings, in-class coaching, growth plans, and continuing coursework with advanced techniques to address a variety of teacher learners. Just like student instruction, some teachers will develop mastery at lower levels of intensity. However, to ensure high levels of fidelity, the most intensive professional development models are necessary. Joyce and Showers (1981) examined the effect of various professional development steps in terms of knowledge mastery, skill mastery, and on-the-job application. Naturally, we expect on-the-job application to be in the best interest of students. In the context of intervention, here is how we define levels of professional development:

Level 1

Level 1 professional development is referred to as "sit and get." There is nothing wrong with this; however, its purpose should be restricted to a preview of coming attractions. Very little of what educators derive from a workshop on theory, or an overview, will find its way into classroom practice—only between two to five percent. If the entire course lasts no more than four hours, consider it Level 1 professional development.

Level 2

Level 2 professional development includes modeling or demonstration of the practices. In a Level 2 setting, the presenter typically uses the participants as students. Often participants watch an instructional model and think it looks easy. Left with a visual demonstration, educators actually implement five to 10 percent of the information from Level 2 professional development into classroom practice. Some Level 2 professional development can last for days. Take note of the engagement level in the next Level 2 professional development. How many people are truly engaged? How many are grading papers?

Tier 3

Tier 3 professional development is intense and can be a bit uncomfortable. Level 3 professional development involves reproduction. The teaching and learning paradigm is, "I do, we do, you do." Elements of Level 1 and Level 2 professional development exist, but the participants must stand and deliver. Level 3 professional development provides the participants time to practice delivering the new technique, skills, or strategy in a safe place: among their peers. Level 3 professional development also allows the facilitator the opportunity to assess his or her own instruction and adjust when necessary. The facilitator in Level 3 also provides feedback, both praising and correcting, to the participants when they show what they know. Depending on the content to be addressed, Level 3 professional development may last for a day, several days, or even a full week. Surprisingly, only about 15 percent of the Level 3 professional development makes it into the classroom practice.

Practitioner's Perspective

This summer, I was delivering Level 3 professional development to a group of teachers. They had reached the first point where they had to teach something back to me. It was quickly evident that I had failed to adequately provide instruction. More than half of the group had not understood. Just like in Tier 3 RTI, I had to assess the failure, revise the instructional delivery, and present the content in a more explicit way. For my second attempt, I broke down my topic into smaller components and checked for mastery much more frequently.

Check Yourself

- Using the definitions described, into what level would I place my previous professional development experiences?

- Did these courses fulfill their espoused purposes?

- How much of what I learned translated into instructional practice?

Level 4

Professional development involves in-class coaching. The most extensive model involves the coach observing the lesson delivery at the teacher's side during an entire period of instruction. The coach provides explicit, targeted intervention at every point of instruction, even interrupting the lesson if necessary. This is difficult to implement without undermining the authority of the teacher. Level 4 professional development requires that teachers receive instruction through Level 3 first, before working with an expert. The results of Level 4 professional development can be stunning, though. With willing participants, 90 percent of instruction through Level 4 transfers to teaching. Naturally, student learning outcomes are similarly impacted. Prepare a plan for your next professional development using the chart below (figure 9.1).

Theory to Practice

Fig. 9.1. Evaluate Professional Development

Workshop	Purpose/Goal	Level 1, 2, 3, or 4	Outcomes for Instructional Practice	Next Steps

Changing Our Frame of Reference

As educators, we need to examine a number of our practices to be sure we are doing our best to serve our culturally diverse populations. A number of changes may need to be made. Some have to do with how we teach. That shift will help to eliminate *dysteachia*. Other changes involve our spoken and unspoken expectations. That will work to eliminate the soft bigotry of low expectations. While one PLC team focuses on professional development, the job of another may be to monitor the culture of the school. If the school makes a dramatic shift in pedagogy, the job of this PLC team becomes even more important.

Returning to the theories of *dysteachia* and the soft bigotry of low expectations, a student's success in the classroom is predicated on their willingness to embrace the notion of curriculum and the practice of instruction as promoted by the teacher (Keddie 1971). Changing the lexicon of classroom instruction is the easy part. The CA-RTI model calls for increasingly explicit instruction as students are placed in Tiers 2 and 3. The language of instruction moves from implicit to explicit, as shown in figure 9.2.

Keep in mind, two curricula work in every school: the formal curriculum and the hidden curriculum. The formal curriculum is the one we practice openly and overtly. It comes from the purchased materials, texts, workbooks, and technology that we use to address the standards. More covert is the hidden curriculum. Sometimes the formal curriculum reflects the ideals and beliefs of those who are most disconnected from the students they serve. When students do not succeed, the hidden curriculum supports the formal curriculum by blaming the failure on genetics, heredity, and culture. The hidden curriculum must be exposed and changed. Students who do successfully learn the formal curriculum do so only after they have overcome the hidden one. What if the hidden curriculum fostered a positive message instead?

Fig. 9.2. The Language of Instruction

Common, non-explicit instructional terms and phrases	Common explicit instructional terms and phrases
Encourage students to identify…	I'm going to show…
Challenge students to say…	My turn to say…
Help students focus on…	Let's say…together
Work with students to build…	See how I make…
Explore…with students	Watch me…
Help students discover…	This is…
Facilitate learning in…	Now you try…on your own
Support success with…	Good job on…

By changing our own mindset, we replace a blame-ridden hidden curriculum with a powerful message of no excuses. Charge the PLC to build a culture of academic achievement for all by exposing and redefining the hidden curriculum. Make it transparent; give it definition. Transmit the definition to the students. Demand that a positive message be communicated to students by all who serve them in the school community. Strong leaders can create a new breed of school. In these schools, the hidden curriculum is not hidden, nor is it harmful. It may even be explicitly acknowledged.

The school that embraces a CA-RTI model must have as its underpinnings an informal curriculum supporting the following beliefs:

- All students can learn.

- Every teacher can reach and teach every child.

- Strong leadership promotes school-wide success.

A curriculum that reflects the three beliefs above has no reason to hide. Achievement for all children becomes the culture of the school. This curriculum promises to take students from where they are to where they need to be. No one is left behind for failing to meet some stereotypical idea of what it means to be a student. Students thrive in a CA-RTI implementation because it fits their needs. Students become lifelong learners, exude model citizenship, and are launched upon a trajectory of success and societal contribution. Isn't this preferable to students who are recipients of societal welfare and victims of the ramifications of asocial behaviors?

Conquering the Master Schedule

The time involved for a successful CA-RTI implementation often raises the affective filter. Whether in elementary, middle, or high school, there is a plan out there for finding the instructional time necessary to implement with fidelity. Granted, elementary school is easier than middle school; and, middle school is easier than high school. However, the first step no matter the grade level is to answer a few simple questions.

- How many, or what percentage of students are at each tier?

- How much time is currently available for daily instruction?

- If students must be brought to grade level in two years, how much do they need to learn within each year?

- How much time can we find for appropriate daily instruction?

- In which domain(s) does instruction need to focus?

- How many instructors are available to serve students? Is this enough?

- In the high school, is there coursework that can be postponed for a year or two to free up time in the master schedule for Tier 2 and Tier 3 instruction?

- In elementary school, how can the school-wide schedule be structured across grades to facilitate intervention that occurs on campus and in a timely manner?

Notice the word *daily* in those questions. It may not be possible to implement a full model in the first year, but consider something before school, after school, or during summer school. A true model requires daily instruction. Students do not grow the gap after school, or only on Mondays and Wednesdays. They grow the gap hour by hour, day by day, and year by year in the present instructional setting. You cannot expect to close it by providing an hours' worth of intervention after school three days each week on a volunteer basis. That just will not do.

A Long Range Plan

Time is a critical element. You cannot restructure for CA-RTI without seriously considering a number of time-related issues. You will have to fundamentally change the way you conceptualize time (Cambone 1995). More than just instructional time, there is political time. Consider the amount of time needed from the governing powers to purchase curriculum, get budgetary approval, and provide staff development. There is also phenomenological time. Remember those roadblocks and pitfalls? It may take some time to overcome obstacles. But it also takes time to plan, not just for one year, but for the next year as well.

The implementation of your CA-RTI model cannot be achieved overnight. A solid implementation model should be built on a three-year calendar. Take your time. Do it right. Provide a plan for strong monitoring and adjust as necessary to confirm your success.

Addressing scheduling concerns may need to begin with central planning that works to eliminate poor articulation and alignment of curriculum between the elementary and middle grades and decreases the risk of academic failure for students already at risk. Central planning is considered an essential component to effective change models in education (Fullan 2002).

Some may argue that central planning eliminates innovation. However, any systemic change or implementation requires a central plan. Your CA-RTI model is innovation. You need a plan that considers where students are coming from and where they need to go. Articulation and alignment must consider all inputs. Central planning should also work to eliminate further creative interpretation of the CA-RTI model once implemented.

Schools are sometimes inclined to go full force in year one. Instead, consider CA-RTI for reading in the first two years. That will allow you to monitor data and adjust instruction. Just as a good scientific investigation adjusts one variable at a time, you will get more valid information about your progress by choosing only one subject area per year for your CA-RTI implementation. The choice of content area on which you focus your phased-in implementation should provide the greatest impact in student learning in each year. Try reading and language curricula to begin in year one. A solid foundation in reading provides for instrumental gains in the area which most impacts learning across the curriculum. In year two, mathematics should be implemented.

With reading securely in place, and teachers more technically proficient with CA-RTI processes and new methodology, effective mathematics instruction will provide the second largest stimulus to raise achievement scores on standardized assessments. The third year curriculum will be dependent on the level of school—primary, middle, or secondary—and the specific needs for improvement. Generally, content-area curriculum and instruction are targeted in year three. Each year, professional development should focus on the specifics of the curricular area being introduced as well as behavior management strategies. In year three, professional development may shift towards advanced teaching techniques.

Not only does a three-year phase-in allow for steady progress, it asks naysayers to suspend judgment. Data suggests that first year gains may be modest. Conley (2005) recommends reporting data over at least a three-year period. You must allow for a lag in the results of the implementation due to factors such as professional development of teachers and teacher fidelity to implementation. This is particularly true if the CA-RTI model or the Tier 2 and 3 curriculum are not fully supported or teachers are not held accountable to implement with fidelity.

Baby Steps and the Implementation Dip

The changes to a CA-RTI implementation will not occur without hindrance. Fullan (2002) warns of a first year filled with implementation challenges, an "implementation dip." To reduce or avoid the implementation dip, participate in a strong professional learning community and begin implementing in-class coaching. Level 4 professional development coaching supports rapid transfer of new skills. Learning within the context of the classroom setting supports and targets your own students; this is preferable to simply observing what others have done in different settings.

Conclusion

The professional learning community is an essential component of the CA-RTI implementation and especially essential for success. Whether you are working on your own or as part of a grade level group of two or three teachers, you are your PLC. Starting small, you have greater flexibility, but you also have some constraints not addressed here. If you are part of a larger organization, a school- or district-wide implementation, the PLC will grow in size, diversity, and specialization of teams. That specialization allows for skilled, focused groups to support targeted professional development, scheduling, and reculturing that must occur for implementations of larger size and scope to enjoy fidelity and success.

Reflect and Act

Work with a colleague, or address the following issues with your administration. Be ready to open up some tough dialogue in three areas:

1. What is common planning time? Do teachers have an adequate amount of common planning time built into the schedule? What are the advantages of a regularly scheduled meeting time? Why does this time need to be separate from a department or faculty meeting?

2. Reflect on your matriculation or vertical teams: Do you know the expectations of the grade-level team above yours? Have you communicated your expectations to the grade level below yours?

3. Evaluate your existing professional development: What are the areas where you and your colleagues need additional support? How do you know? What level of support would be most appropriate?

Chapter 10

Doing RTI Well

We conclude our journey with a look at implementation monitoring. It is vital to ask: Are we doing the right thing? Are we doing it well? Are we doing enough of the right thing to affect the change we're looking for?

Consider the testimony of Colin Shrosbree:

"Middle-class attitudes, middle-class clothes, middle-class accents, early and irrevocable selection by middle-class teachers who made little concession to working-class ways or children's circumstances all made of education a barrier, not just to academic success but to a sense of owning a place in our own culture. But as children we did not question these social divisions—school was just a place apart, with different rules and alien ways, that had no place in our personal or family life."

—*Meira Levinson (2002, 90)*

From what culture is the child quoted above? What might be his home language? Is it apparent in what region of the country he resides? Is it urban, suburban, or rural? In what century did this take place? The quote above could come from any of our CLDLs. The child could come from any number of cultures. Without linguistic features that point to a specific home language, it is difficult to tell what the home language might be. We can glean from the content that this was not a middle-class child, and his home culture was diverse from the culture of school. But who is Colin Shrosbree? Levinson describes Colin not as linguistically diverse, but culturally diverse in that he was from a working-class family, but he attended a private school on scholarship. We must refocus on the culturally and linguistically diverse learner, and realize that this student may or may not look "diverse."

Do the Right Thing

Standards alone cannot improve teaching and learning. Just as it takes a village to raise a child, it takes a community of educators with a shared goal to reform, restructure, and reculture a school. Only then can instruction reach all students, taking them from where they are to where they should be. A culturally appropriate response to intervention (CA-RTI) model provides the framework, and the plan, to do just that.

As educators, we should honor and aspire to what is best for society as well as the individual within the educational setting. We must choose what is right for our students.

The growth of the English language learner population in American schools outpaces any other growth. Thus, these students' impact on school achievement is vital to schools meeting the accountability provisions of No Child Left Behind, and competing for Race to the Top. While these mandates may be revised, it likely will not lower the bar on accountability or achievement. According to the National Clearinghouse for English Language Acquisition (2008), the sole source of growth in the K–12 population in U.S. schools is English language learners. In addition, English language learner subgroups no longer concentrate in the West and Southwest; almost all states now feel the impact of this rapidly growing and culturally diverse group of students.

Teachers who feel unprepared to teach culturally and linguistically diverse students must receive additional training and ongoing support. In addition, curriculum must be developed and implemented that takes into consideration the linguistic processes of developing language and the teaching of core content to CLDL students. The CA-RTI model targets this specific demographic. Secondly, researchers have recently indicated that the normal frequency of true cognitive disability is only three to five percent of the population. The new regulations under the Individuals with Disabilities in Education Act (IDEA) should motivate schools to change the model of identification from the "wait to fail" model to the "response to intervention" model. More than ever before, the general education classroom provides the services for the special education student, as well as the potential special education student. Those teachers not adequately prepared to provide intervention and remediation for students who do not progress at normal rates will benefit from coaching and professional development.

Check Yourself

- What is the rate of referral to special education for CLDLs in my school? My district?

- What is the dropout rate for culturally and linguistically diverse learners in my school? (The CA-RTI model is designed to reduce those rates.)

The adoption of the Common Core Curriculum Standards will play a key role in curriculum change. The Common Core Standards reflect the fact that we live in a transient society. As our society has become more and more mobile, it is up to the schools to change to reflect that mobility. Students, especially those at risk, require consistency of skills expectations and benchmarks. If the standards are nationalized, the approach to teaching to the standards must lead to a reliance on scientific evidence in teaching and learning to guide instruction. For example, although the provisions of NCLB were clearly defined, program design and implementation were not as clear. It is not enough to label a student *proficient* or *basic*, particularly when those terms reflect a moving target of skill proficiency. If a student is proficient in one state, why is he or she below basic in another? As educators, we are builders. We all have the same raw material: children. If the building code is nationalized, a mansion in one state would not be considered a tenement slum in another.

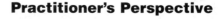

Practitioner's Perspective

The politics and processes of K–12 education, particularly public education, are dynamic. We stated that implementation of CA-RTI should be seen as a three-year process. In planning, consider what additional changes in curriculum may transpire over those three years. I am no Nostradamus, but in 2006, I made some projections about what I anticipated for education in the coming years (Berry 2006). I included ideas ranging from standards-based instruction to the politics of curriculum content and implementation. As a history teacher, I find that looking back helps me see the present with greater clarity. Hindsight is 20/20. I share these with you so that you consider what has shaped and what will continue to shape the educational experiences of children at-risk in urban, public schools. In 2006, I ranked the following statements according to their impact on the educational system, based on what I knew at the time:

1. *The rapid growth of the population of English language learners and the effect on school achievement.*

2. *The increased inclusion of special education students in the general education classroom.*

3. *The nationalization of standards in core content areas.*

4. *The reliance of scientific evidence in teaching and learning to guide program development.*

5. *The use of assessment and accountability to guide instruction.*

6. *The increased use of technology across the curriculum.*

At the time, I considered these six elements to serve as the impetus for any changes to come. Some of these were fledgling ideas and have become more accepted as norms. None of these factors has lost significance.

The CA-RTI model will provide the school with tools and skills to reflect on instruction based on data, and adjust as necessary.

The CA-RTI model supports the use of assessment and accountability to guide instruction. Where teachers assess, and use the data to drive instruction, students have greater opportunities for, and successes at, learning.

Technology has a place in teaching and learning, and it can play a prominent role in CA-RTI, but it cannot replace the teacher. It can supplement, but not supplant the teacher's instruction. However, I also believe the increased use of technology across the curriculum will be compelled by the drive towards differentiation. As you consider the factors above, use them not only to guide your plan of implementation, but how you monitor that implementation. Look at the changes in demographics that affect your school.

Do the Right Thing Well

Doing the right thing works best when the right thing is done well. Monitor the fidelity of CA-RTI instruction. One PLC team should be charged with monitoring instructional delivery, progress, lesson completion, and data. Scientifically validated programs must be implemented with complete fidelity. Scientifically based programs may be "beefed up" to increase the rigor. The fidelity of instruction is critical. Work to eliminate teacher creativity that hinders student performance. Low fidelity results in insufficient outcomes. Closing the gap requires consistency of both teacher and student performance.

In both developing and monitoring the fidelity of your CA-RTI implementation, you must identify the causes for student performance below Tier 1. You must also consider solutions to address those causes. Revisit the core instruction. Is it working? Are you narrowing the gap? Why or why not? Corrective action can be harsh and result in unintended consequences. If CA-RTI is effectively and successfully implemented, you may avoid corrective action. If you are already taking corrective action, you may be able to expedite the process. Remember, CA-RTI may be primarily about the students, but it is through increased instructional and organizational efficiency that its results are achieved.

Simply put, doing the right thing well consists of analyzing student academic achievement gaps systematically, identifying the root causes of the gaps, considering various scientifically validated (or based) solutions to address the gaps, and implementing those scientifically validated (or scientifically based) solutions to close the gap. The chief aim, then, would be to improve teacher performance to increase instructional efficiency and effectiveness.

Standards have worked to improve curriculum, instruction, and assessment in the K–12 educational environment in a number of ways. Most standards reflect the most recent research. Well-developed standards offer guidance for teachers in determining the appropriateness of instruction for their students. Vertically- and horizontally-aligned standards provide a framework for teachers to articulate instruction across and between grade levels. Standards provide a clear and uniform foundation for assessment. Finally, standards-based assessments provide a mechanism for assessment-driven instruction (Conley 2005).

Doing the right thing well requires an examination of the human element. Teachers must be committed to success with the CA-RTI model and demonstrate technical proficiency with the instructional tools and curricula used in each tier. Lack of commitment and lack of proficiency contribute directly to the failure of schools. This is particularly true when schools lack instructional resources, lack sufficient instructors, and lack instructors with sufficient technical knowledge. In addition, the high turnover of principals and teachers can quickly cause the implementation to fail. Build a team. Support it. To self-monitor as you develop, and to monitor throughout the implementation, use the rubric in figure 10.1 to gauge your own CA-RTI instructional model compliance.

Fig. 10.1. CA-RTI Instructional Model Compliance

Criteria	Evidence in Plan/Practice		
	No (0 points)	Somewhat (1 point)	Yes (2 points)
Students are grouped/regrouped according to data			
Tier 2 and Tier 3 groups are homogeneous			
There is 90–120 minutes of daily core literacy instruction for students at Tier 1 and Tier 2			
Tier 2 students have an additional 30 minutes of daily intervention			
Tier 3 students have 90–120 minutes of daily instruction in an alternate (Tier 3) core (the Tier 1 core is supplanted)			
Tier 2 and Tier 3 groups are small; they are sized appropriate to the grade level, intensity level, and curriculum suggestions (for commercial curricula)			
The most highly qualified teachers work with the most at-risk students			
Additional personnel are identified to facilitate the instruction of students in small groups			
Appropriate intervention curriculum based on assessment and screening data have been identified within the plan to address the needs of intervention students			
Initial and ongoing professional development to support the instructional model is identified			

The maximum score on the rubric for three-tiered instructional model compliance is 20. Investigate any item scored at zero.

Score

20/20	Awesome! You are restructured, recultured, and changing the life trajectories of your students.
17–19/20	You are on the right track. Choose one critical element on which to focus for improvement.
15–16/20	Good job getting started. Prioritize your weaknesses and develop a plan to address them.
0–14/20	Nice job recognizing that there is work to be done. What is the most pressing problem to address? You may need to review a few chapters, or charge a PLC team with the task of solidifying your plan.

Do Enough of the Right Thing to Affect Change

For the next several exercises, reflect back on the Theory to Practice activity in Chapter 2 (page 42). As an RTI plan is developed, use some basic guiding questions based on both a qualitative (characteristic or philosophical) perspective and a quantitative (measurable) perspective. These should facilitate planning that will move instruction in Tiers 2 and 3 towards a more explicit approach.

1. What is the current core instructional program?

2. Where does the core lie on the pedagogical spectrum?

3. Which RTI curricula, either already in place or under consideration, are further to the right of the core on the pedagogical spectrum?

4. How much more intense is the implementation likely to get?

Be aware of two critical issues. First, too dramatic a shift may result in pushback from stakeholders who have a vested interest or strong philosophical allegiance to the approach or curriculum presently in place at Tier 1. Second, a shift to a less explicit instructional method will not produce positive outcomes. Students will not progress to benchmark by doing less.

In Chapter 9, eight questions were posed to help establish the framework for conquering the master schedule (page 168). Those eight questions asked for quantifiable, numeric data. Four of those questions are critical to monitoring as well as planning. With quantitative data, your plan has a realistic design based on hard facts. When you answered these questions the first time, it was about the schedule. The four questions below should help you determine how explicit the curricula must be to achieve the school's goals and close the gap. With this information, you can examine programs and methods that are designed to meet the needs of the students based on specific, measurable criteria and outcomes.

1. How low are the students?

2. How much time is available for daily instruction?

3. If students must be brought to grade level in two years, how much do they need to learn within one year?

4. How much time can be committed for appropriate daily instruction?

Theory to Practice

Use these exercises to keep your CA-RTI model strong.

Exercise 1

As you review the pedagogical spectrum you created back in Chapter 2, take this as an extension activity. In developing your CA-RTI plan and selecting curriculum for each of the tiers, be able to list the evidence for using the proposed curriculum at that tier. If selecting a commercial curriculum, ask for the scientific validation studies. Consider the explicit and systematic, scientifically validated, core instruction for CLDLs. Consider the necessary instruction in expressive and receptive language for CLDLs. Keep in mind the evidence for early instruction in phonemic awareness, phonics, and fluency for ELLs and CLDLs. In completing this exercise, an inductive exposition approach is recommended. Think-pair-share activities, or jigsawing research articles for rapid reading and discussion in small groups prior to whole group discussion will facilitate the dissemination of information and lead to greater coverage of the topic and the ability for all to share knowledge. One important task of the PLC is to transfer knowledge gained throughout the community of stakeholders.

Exercise 2

Using the instructional materials in place at present, plug them in to the CA-RTI frame. See what you presently have that appropriately addresses the needs of Tier 1, Tier 2, and Tier 3 learners, including your CLDLs at each level. You might find it easier to break this exercise down into subsections depending on the curriculum to be examined. The PLC team must take into account the level of experience with each curriculum or curriculum component and ELD teaching strategies.

Exercise 3

Using the beginning of year, middle of year, and end of year progress monitoring data, write or review your CA-RTI plan for the upcoming school year. Include data analysis, technical compliance, and professional development needs in order for the school's population to have a minimum of 85% of students at benchmark, no more than 10% of students at strategic, and no more than 5% of students at intensive by the end of the third year of implementation.

Persistency, Consistency, Discipline, and Focus

Never underestimate the power of the determined. That is a mantra to live by. The book *No Excuses* (Carter 2000) outlines 21 lessons learned from observing the leadership in high-performing schools that are also high poverty. In those schools, there is a climate of achievement that is not found in other schools with similar high-poverty demographics. At the schools described in his book, the informal curriculum connects to the CA-RTI model.

First, principals charged with improving outcomes must have the freedom to structure learning environments that work for their students. In the CA-RTI model, language must be addressed not only for English language learners, but school English learners as well. If providing English language development for all students will improve achievement, why should only the identified English language learners receive it? Second, principals must use measurable goals to establish a culture of achievement. It is not enough to merely settle for making AYP; blow the socks off the neighboring schools! Third, employ master teachers to bring out the best in a faculty. Many of us have experienced being in schools with tremendous *esprit de corps*. The support of a master teacher can sustain a positive lexicon in practice and belief. Just like students experiencing success, when teachers do the right thing, do it well, and get supported, they shine.

Although no one likes tests, rigorous and regular testing leads to continuous student achievement. Life is filled with measurements. You cannot bake a cake without measuring some ingredients. You need assessments to determine whether what you are teaching is actually being learned. Benchmarks and trajectories, goals and aims, these all drive continuous achievement. The CA-RTI assessment round and progress monitoring provisions assure that focus on a positive trajectory of growth is maintained.

Practitioner's Perspective

David was convinced I did not know how to interpret his reading assessment, and it was my shortcoming that resulted in his placement into intervention. David was about two years below grade level at the beginning of the year. David rebelled against all of my strict disciplinary measures at every opportunity. Upon entering class, he would not remove his hat. He tipped his chair. But one day in class we played a game that pitted the students against the teacher. This gave the students motivation to practice good behavior during each lesson, and it kept me on my toes remembering to deliver behavioral praise. Every time I noticed the class as a whole did something behaviorally correct, I awarded them two points. Every time one individual violated a rule, I gave myself one point. To win, the students had to beat me by ten points. It didn't take long for the other students to "assist" David with removing his hat. They helped him push in his chair. They adjusted his materials and personal belongings. In time, David got with the program. In fact, he began to excel academically and behaviorally. His daily scores ranged between 95 and 100 percent, precisely where intervention scores need to be. And his behavior shifted dramatically, for the better. I live in California, where students do not automatically address adults as "sir" or "ma'am." However, that was the expectation in my classroom. One day there were not enough substitutes on campus, so some students were placed in other classrooms. A visiting student attempted to get my attention by yelling, "Hey!" David wouldn't hear of it. He immediately redressed the student, explaining that I was to be called by "Ma'am" or "Ms. Berry," and that the student was to raise his hand and wait patiently until recognized. You see, David was only a discipline problem when he was unsuccessful.

Conclusion

Finally, effort creates ability. The more we do well, the easier doing well becomes. The easier it becomes, the better we do. You will work hard to develop, implement, and maintain your CA-RTI implementation. But the harder you work, the easier it will become. The easier it becomes, and the better results you attain, the more you will be willing to work hard. The same is true of the students. When the instruction works for them, rather than against them, the more they are willing to work. When they recognize their hard work is paying off, they will continue to put forth the effort to increase their ability and, therefore, their success.

In Carter's *No Excuses* schools, 75 percent or more of the students are Title I (low-income), yet school-wide median test scores were all above the 65th percentile on national academic achievement tests. Schools with similar demographics typically have median test scores below the 35th percentile (Carter 2000). So get rid of the excuses. Accept nothing less than the best. Approach the implementation of CA-RTI with persistency, consistency, discipline, and focus, and you will change lives.

Reflect and Act

1. Work with your PLC or a colleague and complete the Theory to Practice exercises on page 182. What kind of action plan can you put in place right away? How can you plan long-term?

2 Have a conversation with your site administrator about intervention. Is there a teacher leader who could work with you to improve intervention practices at your school? Is that person you?

References

Abedi, J. 2004. The No Child Left Behind Act and English language learners: Assessment and accountability issues. *Educational Researcher* 33 (1):4–14.

Argüelles, M. E. 2005. *Components of effective reading instruction for English language learners.* Paper presented at the National Reading First Conference, New Orleans.

August, D., and T. Shanahan, eds. 2006. *Developing literacy in second-language learners: Report of the National Literacy Panel on language-minority children and youth.* Mahwah, NJ: Lawrence Erlbaum Associates.

Balfanz, R., and N. Legters. 2004. *Locating the dropout crisis: Which high schools produce the nation's dropouts? Where are they located? Who attends them?* (Report 70). Baltimore, MD: Johns Hopkins University, Center for Research on the Education of Students Placed At Risk.

Bandura, A. 1991. Social cognitive theory of moral thought and action. In *Handbook of moral behavior and development,* vol. 1, Eds. W. M. Kurtines and J. L. Gewirtz, 45–103. Hillsdale, NJ: L. Erlbaum.

Beck, I. L., M. G. McKeown, and L. Kucan. 2002. *Bringing words to life: Robust vocabulary instruction.* New York: Guilford Press.

Beglau, M. 2005. Can technology narrow the black-white achievement gap? *THE Journal* 32 (12):13–17.

Berninger, V. W., R. D. Abbott, H. Swanson, D. Lovitt, P. Trivedi, S. Lin, et al. 2010. Relationship of word- and sentence-level working memory to reading and writing in second, fourth, and sixth grade. *Language, Speech and Hearing Services in Schools* 41 (2):179–193. Retrieved from CINAHL Plus with Full Text database.

Berninger, V. W., R. D. Abbott, K. Vermeulen, and C. M. Fulton. 2006. Paths to reading comprehension in at-risk second-grade readers. *Journal of Learning Disabilities* 39 (4):334–351.
http://www.hammill-institute.org/journals/JLD.html

Berry, A. L. 2006. *Trends in curriculum through 2016: What we can expect in urban education.* Unpublished manuscript.

Beswick, J. F., J. D. Willms, and E. A. Sloat. 2005. A comparative study of teacher ratings of emergent literacy skills and student performance on a standardized measure. *Education* 126 (1):116–137.

Biemiller, A. 1999. *Language and reading success.* Newton Upper Falls, MA: Brookline Books.

Boeree, C. G. 1998, 2006. *Personality theories.* Albert Bandura. http://www.ship.edu/7Ecgboeree/bandura.html.

Borman, G. D., G. M. Hewes, L. T. Overman, and S. Brown. 2002. *Comprehensive school reform and student achievement: A meta-analysis.* (Report No. 59). Baltimore, MD: John Hopkins University, Center for the Education of Students Placed at Risk.

Brady, S., and L. C. Moats. 1997. *Informed instruction for reading success: Foundations for teacher preparation.* Paper presented at the International Dyslexia Association Conference, Baltimore, MD: International Dyslexia Association, March.

Britton, P., J. Brooks-Gunn, and T. M. Griffin. January/February/March, 2006. Maternal reading and teaching patterns: Associations with school readiness in low-income African American families. *Reading Research Quarterly* 41(1): 68–89.

Byrne, B., and R. Fielding-Barnsley. 1995. Evaluation of a program to teach phonemic awareness to young children: A 2- and 3-year follow-up and a new preschool trial. *Journal of Educational Psychology* 87 (3):488–503.

Cambone, J. 1995. Time for teachers in school restructuring. *Teachers College Record* 96 (3): 512–543

Carlson, C. D., and D. J. Francis. 2002. Increasing the reading achievement of at-risk children through direct instruction: Evaluation of the rodeo institute for teacher excellence (RITE). *Journal of Education for Students Placed At Risk* 7 (2):141–166.

Carnine, D. 2000. *Why education experts resist effective practices (And what it would take to make education more like medicine).* Washington, DC: Thomas B. Fordham Foundation. http://www.edexcellence.net (Accessed April 16, 2008.)

Carter, S. C. 2000. *No excuses: Lessons from 21 high-performing, high-poverty schools.* Washington, DC: The Heritage Foundation.

Causey-Bush, T. 2005. Keep your eye on Texas and California: A look at testing, school reform, No Child Left Behind, and implications for students of color. *Journal of Negro Education* 74 (4):332–343.

Chamberlain, S. P. 2005. Recognizing and responding to cultural differences in the education of culturally and linguistically diverse learners. *Intervention in School and Clinic* 40 (4):195–211.

Children of the Code: A Social Education Project. The history and science of the code and what is at stake and involved in learning to read it. *Learning Stewards,* a 501(c)(3) Non-Profit Organization. http://www.chidrenofthecode.org/

Cohen, C., N. Deterding, and B.C. Clewell. 2005. *Who's left behind? Immigrant children in high and low LEP schools.* Washington, DC: The Urban Institute.

Collier, V. P. (1995). Acquiring a second language for school. *Directions in Language & Education* 1:1–8.

Conley, M. W. 2005. *Connecting standards and assessment through literacy.* Boston: Pearson/Allyn and Bacon.

Cummins, J. 1979. Cognitive/academic language proficiency, linguistic interdependence, the optimum age question and some other matters. *Working Papers on Bilingualism* 19:121–129.

———. 1984. Wanted: A theoretical framework for relating language proficiency to academic achievement among bilingual students. In *Language proficiency and academic achievement.* Ed. C. Rivera, 2–19.

DeBell, M., and C. Chapman. 2006. *Computer and internet use by students in 2003.* (NCES 2006-065). U.S. Department of Education. Washington, DC: National Center for Education Statistics. Available at http://nces.ed.gov/pubs2006/2006065.pdf.

DeMarrais, K. B., and M. D. LeCompte. 1999. *The way schools work: A sociological analysis of education.* 3rd ed. New York: Longman.

The Education Trust. 2003. "Don't turn back the clock!" *Over 100 African American and Latino superintendents voice their support for the accountability provisions in Title I (NCLB).* November 18. http://www.edtrust.org/dc/press-room/press-release/donE28099t-turn-back-the-clockE2809D-over-100-african-american-and-latino-superint.

Ehri, L. C., and L.S. Wilce. 1983. Development of word identification speed in skilled and less skilled beginning readers. *Journal of Educational Psychology* 75 (1):3–18.

Elbaum, B., S. Vaughn, M. Hughes, and S. W. Moody. 1999. Grouping practice and reading outcomes for students with disabilities. *Exceptional Children* 65 (3):399–415.

Engelmann, S. 2006. How scientific is Reading First? *Direct Instruction News,* Spring, 15–17.

———. 2008. *Preventing failure in the primary grades.* Eugene, OR: Association for Direct Instruction.

Engelmann, S. and J. Osborn. 2008. *Language for Learning.* Columbus, OH: SRA-McGraw-Hill.

Foorman, B. R., and L. C. Moats. 2004. Conditions for sustaining research-based practices in early reading instruction. *Remedial and Special Education* 25 (1):51–60.

Francis, D. J. 2005. *Developing language and literacy in English language learners: Research, practice, and partnerships.* Presentation to Brownsville Independent School District Board of Education. Brownsville, TX.

Frey, B. B., S. W. Lee, N. Tollefson, L. Pass, and D. Massengill. 2005. Balanced literacy in an urban school district. *Journal of Educational Research* 98 (5):272–280.

Fullan, M. 2000. The three stories of education reform. *Phi Delta Kappan* 81
———. 2002. The change leader. *Educational Leadership* 59 (8):16.

Gant, V. T. 2005. The economics of school choice. *Journal of Education* 186 (2):1–8.

Gersten, R., D. W. Carnine, and P. B. Williams. 1982. Measuring implementation of a structured educational model in an urban school district: An observational approach. *Educational Evaluation and Policy Analysis* 4(1):67–79.

Gersten, R., and E. Geva. 2003. Teaching reading to early language learners. *Educational Leadership* 60 (7):44–49.

Gersten, R., T. Keating, and W. C. Becker. 1988. The continued impact of the direct instruction model: Longitudinal studies of follow through students. *Education and Treatment of Children* 11(4): 318–327

Gersten, R., M. Morvant, and S. Brengelman. 1995. Close to the classroom is close to the bone: Coaching as a means to translate research into classroom practice. *Exceptional Children* 62 (1):52–66.

Gersten, R., S. K. Baker, D. Haager, and A. W. Graves. 2005. Exploring the role of teacher quality in predicting reading outcomes for first-grade English learners: An observational study. *Remedial and Special Education* 26 (4):197–206.

Gersten, R., S. K. Baker, T. Shanahan, S. Linan-Thompson, P. Collins, and R. Scarcella. 2007. *Effective Literacy and English Language Instruction for English Learners in the Elementary Grades: IES Practice Guide* (NCEE 2007-4011). Washington, DC: National Center for Education Evaluation and Regional Assistance, Institute of Education Sciences, U.S. Department of Education. Retrieved from: http://ies.ed.gov/ncee.

Geva, E., and M. Wang. 2001. The development of basic reading skills in children: a cross-language perspective. *Annual Review of Applied Linguistics* 21: 182–204.

Gilbert, G. G. 1981. French and German: *A comparative study*. In *Language in the USA*, ed. C. A. Ferguson, S. B. Heath, and D. Hwang, 257–272. Cambridge: Cambridge University Press.

Golden, M. 2005. Making strides with educational data. *THE Journal* 32 (12):38–40.

Graves, A., and R. Gersten. April, 2002. *Instruction and literacy development of English-language learners: Descriptive research in grade one classrooms*. Presentation at the Council for Exceptional Children Annual Convention, New York.

Greene, J. P. 2002. Graduation statistics: Caveat Emptor. *Education Week* 21 (18):52.

Griffin, M. 1991. Social learning theory of Albert Bandura. In *A First Look at Communication Theory,* 1st ed., 367–376. McGraw-Hill. http://www.mhhe.com/socscience/comm/bandur-s.mhtml (Accessed February, 17, 2008.)

Grossen, B. 2003. *Movement of English language learners into the advanced score range on the California English Language Development Test.* Unpublished raw data.

Gutek, G. L. 1997. *Philosophical and ideological perspectives on education,* 2nd ed. Boston: Allyn and Bacon.

Hall, T. 2008. Doing harm, allowing harm, and denying resources. *Journal of Moral Philosophy* 5 (1):50–76.

Hart, B., and T. R. Risley. 1995. *Meaningful differences in the everyday experience of young American children.* Baltimore: P. H. Brookes.

Hlebowitsh, P. 2005. *Designing the school curriculum.* Boston: Pearson/Allyn and Bacon.

Hoover, W. A., and P. B. Gough. 1990. The simple view of reading. *Reading and Writing: An Interdisciplinary Journal* 2 (2):127–160.

Iaquinta, A. 2006. Guided reading: A research-based response to the challenges of early reading instruction. *Early Childhood Education Journal* 33 (6):413-418. http://www.springerlink.com/content/0p471t4203n4g364/fulltext.html.

Joftus, S., and B. Maddox-Dolan. 2003. *Left out and left behind: NCLB and the American high school.* Washington, DC: Alliance for Excellent Education.

Joyce, B., and B. Showers. 1980. Improving inservice training: The message of research. *Educational Leadership* 37 (5):379–385. Retrieved from Education Research Complete database.

———. 1981. Transfer of training: The contribution of "coaching." *Journal of Education* 163 (2):163–172.

Juel, C. 1988. Learning to read and write: A longitudinal study of 54 children from first through fourth grades. *Journal of Educational Psychology* 80 (4):437–447.

Kame'enui, E. J., L. Fuchs, D. J. Francis, R. Good III, R. E. O'Connor, D. C. Simmons, G. Tindal, and J. K. Torgesen. 2006. The adequacy of tools for assessing reading competence: A framework and review. *Educational Researcher* 35(4):3–11.

Kamps, D., M. Abbott, C. Greenwood, C. Arreaga-Mayer, H. Wills, J. Longstaff, M. Culpepper, C. Walton. 2007. Use of evidence-based, small-group reading instruction for English language learners in elementary grades: Secondary-tier intervention. *Learning Disabilities Quarterly* 30 (3):153–168.

Keddie, N. 1971. Classroom knowledge. In *Knowledge and control: New directions for the sociology of education,* ed. M. F. D. Young, 133–160. London: Collier-Macmillan Publishers.

KewalRamani, A., L. Gilbertson, M. M. Fox, and S. Provasnik. 2007. *Status and Trends in the Education of Racial and Ethnic Minorities* (NCES 2007-039). Washington, DC: National Center for Education Statistics, Institute of Education Sciences, U.S. Department of Education. http://www.eric.ed.gov/PDFS/ED498259.pdf.

Kim, T., and S. Axelrod. 2005. Direct instruction: An educator's guide and a plea for action. *Behavior Analyst Today* 6 (2):111–120.

Krashen, S. D. 1982. *Principles and practice in second language acquisition.* Oxford: Pergamon.

Lasagne, L. 1964. *Hippocratic Oath—Modern Version.* WGBH Educational Foundation for PBS and NOVA Online. http://www.pbs.org/wgbh/nova/doctors/oath_modern.html

Lau v. Nichols, 414 U.S. 563 (1974).

Lee, J., W. Grigg, and P. Donahue. 2007. The nation's report card: Reading 2007 (NCES 2007–496). National Center for Education Statistics, Institute of Education Sciences, U.S. Department of Education, Washington, D.C.

Levinson, M. 2002. *The demands of liberal education.* Oxford: Oxford University Press.

Lewis, T. J., G. Sugai, and G. Colvin. 1999. Effective behavior support: A systems approach to proactive schoolwide management. *Focus on Exceptional Children* 31 (6):1–24.

Linan-Thompson, S., S. Vaughn, P. Hickman-Davis, and K. Kouzekanani. 2003. Effectiveness of supplemental reading instruction for second-grade English language learners with reading difficulties. *Elementary School Journal* 103 (3):221–238.

Marchand-Martella, N. E., T. A. Slocum, and R. C. Martella, eds. 2004. *Introduction to direct instruction.* Boston, MA: Pearson/Allyn and Bacon.

Mathes, P. G., C. A. Denton, J. M. Fletcher, J. L. Anthony, D. J. Francis, and C. Schatschneider. 2005. The effects of theoretically different instruction and student characteristics on the skills of struggling readers. *Reading Research Quarterly* 40(2):148–182.

McCardle, P., H. S. Scarborough, and H. W. Catts. 2001. Predicting, explaining, and preventing children's reading difficulties. *Learning Disabilities: Research and Practice* 16 (4):230–239.

McKay, S. L., and S. C. Wong, eds. 2000. *New immigrants in the United States: Readings for second language educators.* Cambridge: Cambridge University Press.

McLaughlin, B. 1992. Myths and misconceptions about second language learning: What every teacher needs to unlearn. *Educational Practice Report, 5*. National Center for Research on Cultural Diversity and Second Language Learning. Washington D.C: Center for Applied Linguistics.

Myers, L., and N. Botting. 2008. Literacy in the mainstream inner-city school: Its relationship to spoken language. *Child Language Teaching and Therapy* 24 (1):95–114.

National Center for Education Statistics. 2009. The Nation's Report Card: Reading 2009 (NCES 2010–458). Institute of Education Sciences, U.S. Department of Education, Washington, D.C.

National Clearinghouse for English Language Acquisition and Language Instruction Educational Programs. 2008. NCELA. http://www.ncela.gwu.edu/faqs/

National Reading Panel. 2000. *Report of the National Reading Panel: Teaching children to read,* (NIH Publication No. 00–4769). Rockville, MD: National Institute of Child Health and Human Development.

Newport, E. 1990. Maturational constraints on language learning. *Cognitive Science* 14:11–28.

Ogbu, J. 1987. Variability in minority responses to schooling: A problem in search of an explanation. *Anthropology and Education Quarterly*.

Pai, Y., S. A. Adler, and L. Shadiow. 2005. *Cultural foundations of education.* 4th ed. Upper Saddle River, NJ: Pearson/Merrill/Prentice-Hall.

Palincsar, A. S., and A. L. Brown. 1984. Reciprocal teaching of comprehension-fostering and comprehension-monitoring activities. *Cognition and Instruction* 1 (2):117–175.

Perie, M., W. Grigg, and P. Donahue, P. 2005. The Nation's Report Card: Reading 2005 (NCES 2006–451). U.S. Department of Education, National Center for Education Statistics. Washington, D.C.: U.S. Government Printing Office.

Plyler v. Doe, 457 U.S. 202 (1982).

Pray, L. 2005. How well do commonly used language instruments measure English oral-language proficiency? *Bilingual Research Journal* 29 (2):387–411.

Quiroga, T., Z. Lemos-Britton, E. Mostafapour, R. D. Abbott, and V. W. Berninger. 2002. Phonological awareness and beginning reading in Spanish-speaking ESL first graders: Research into practice. *Journal of School Psychology* 40 (1): 85–111.

Richgels, D. 1982. Schema theory, linguistic theory, and representations of reading comprehension. *Journal of Educational Research* 76 (1): 54–61

Roeser, R. W. 2001. To cultivate the positive: Introduction to the special issue on schooling and mental health issues. *Journal of School Psychology* 39: 99–110.

Roeser, R. W., and J. S. Eccles. 2000. Schooling and mental health. In *Handbook of developmental psychopathology*, 2nd ed. Eds. A. J. Sameroff, M. Lewis, and S. M. Miller, 135–156. New York: Kluwer Academic/Plenum.

Scherer, M. 2004. A call for powerful leaders: A conversation with Rod Paige. *Educational Leadership* 61 (7):20–23.

Schunk, D. H. 2004. *Learning theories: An educational perspective.* 4th ed. Upper Saddle River, NJ: Pearson/Merrill/Prentice-Hall.

Shanahan, T. 2005. *How to improve reading achievement: Core teaching and differentiated instruction.* Keynote presented at the Georgia Reading First Conference, Atlanta, GA.

Shaywitz, S. 2003. *Overcoming dyslexia: A new and complete science-based program for reading problems at any level.* New York: A. A. Knopf.

Skinner, C. and E. Smith. 1992. Issues surrounding the use of self-management interventions for increasing academic performance. *School Psychology Review.* 21 (2):202. Retrieved from MasterFILE Premier database.

Slavin, R. E. 2005. *Educational psychology,.* 8th ed. Boston: Allyn and Bacon.

Slavin, R. E., and A. Cheung. 2003. *Effective reading programs for English language learners: A best-evidence synthesis.* (Report No. 66). Baltimore, MD: Center for Research on the Education of Students Placed at Risk.

Slavin, R. E., and O. S. Fashola. 1998. *Show me the evidence! Proven and promising programs for America's schools.* Thousand Oaks, CA: Corwin Press.

Snow, C. E. 1994. What is so hard about learning to read? A pragmatic analysis. In *Pragmatics: From theory to practice,* eds. J. Duchan, R. Sonnemeier, and L. Hewitt (164–184). Englewood Cliffs, NJ: Prentice Hall.

Snow, C. E., S. Burns, and P. Griffin (Eds.) 1998. *Preventing reading difficulties in young children.* National Academy Press: Washington, D.C.

Snow, C., and C. Juel, 2004. Teaching children to read: What do we know about how to do it? In *The Science of Reading: A Handbook,* eds. Snowling, M. J. and Hulme, C. Blackwell Publishing. Blackwell Reference Online. DOI 10.1111/b.9781405114882.2005.

Speece, D. L. *Journal of Special Education* 28 (3):259–274. http://sed.sagepub.com/content/28/3/259.full.pdf+html.

Speece D. L. and K. D. Ritchie. 2005. A longitudinal study of the development or oral reading fluency in young children at risk for reading failure [Electronic version]. *Journal of Learning Disabilities* 38 (5):387–400.

Stanovich, K. E. 2004. *The robot's rebellion: Finding meaning in the age of Darwin.* Chicago, IL: The University of Chicago Press.

Stecker, P. M., L. S. Fuchs, and D. Fuchs. 2005. Using curriculum-based measurement to improve student achievement: *Review of research. Psychology in the Schools* 42:795–820.

Thomas, W. P., and V. P. Collier. 2001. *A national study of school effectiveness for language minority students' long-term academic achievement final report: Project 1.1.* Berkeley, CA: Center for Research on Education, Diversity, and Excellence. http://crede.berkeley.edu/research/llaa/1.1_final.html.

Tivnan, T., and L. Hemphill. 2005. Comparing four literacy reform models in high-poverty schools: Patterns of first-grade achievement. *Elementary School Journal* 105 (5):419–443.

Tozer, S. E., P. C. Violas, and G. Senese. 2002. *School and society: Historical and contemporary perspectives.* 4th ed. Boston: McGraw-Hill.

U.S. Department of Education. 2003. *Nation's report card: Reading 2002.* Washington, D.C.: National Center for Education Statistics.

Watson, John B. 1930. *Behaviorism.* Rev. ed. Chicago: University of Chicago Press.

Wheatley, M., and D. Frieze. 2007. Beyond networking: How large-scale change really happens. *School Administrator* 64 (4):35–38.

Wiley, T. 1998. The imposition of World War I era English-only policies and the fate of Germans in North America. In *Language and Politics in the United States and Canada,* ed. T. Ricento, and B. Burnaby, 211–241. Mahwah, NJ: Lawrence Erlbaum Associates.

Wiley, T. G., and W. E. Wright. 2004. Against the undertow: Language-minority education policy and politics in the "age of accountability." *Educational Policy* 18 (1):142–168.

Wise, J. C., R. A. Sevcik, R. D. Morris, M. W. Lovett, and M. Wolf. 2007. The relationship among receptive and expressive vocabulary, listening comprehension, pre-reading skills, word identification skills, and reading comprehension by children with reading disabilities. *Journal of Speech, Language, and Hearing Research* 50 (4):1093–1109. http://jslhr.asha.org/cgi/content/full/50/4/1093.